THE BEADED BRACELET

Beadweaving Techniques and Patterns for 20 Eye-Catching Projects

By Carole Rodgers

NORTH LIGHT BOOKS
Cincinnati, Ohio

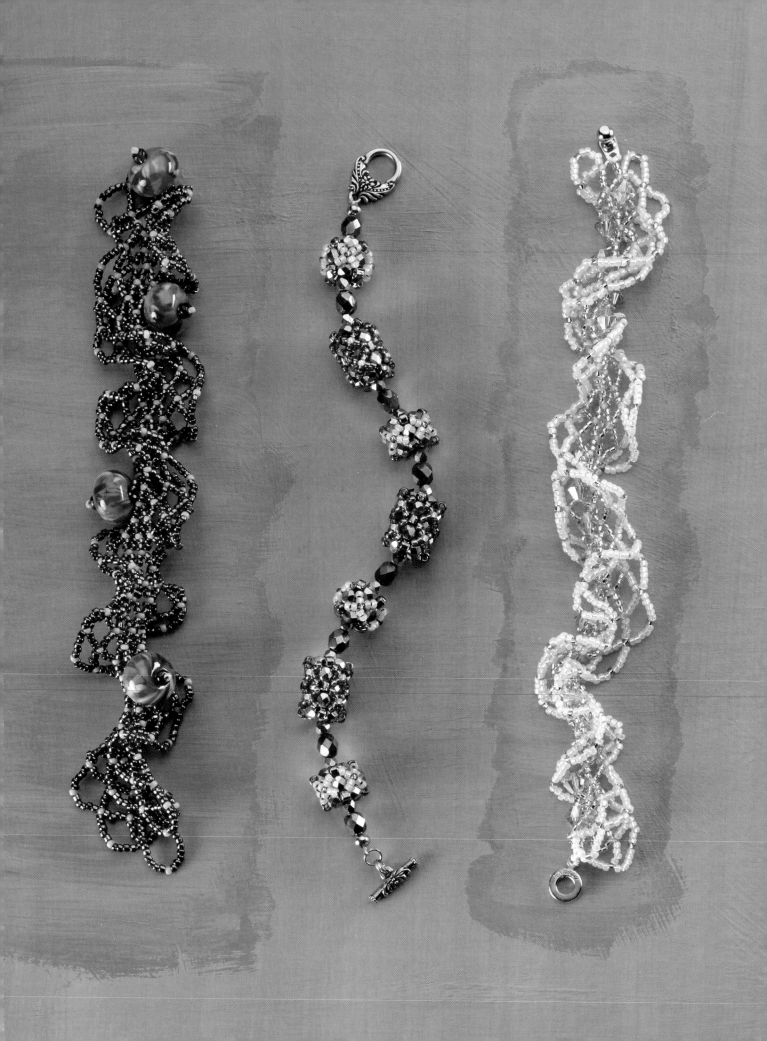

Contents

Introduction

My husband and I do a number of retail bead and rock and gem shows every year as we travel around the country in our recreational vehicle. Over the years I developed a line of kits that we sell at the shows (along with the three books I have written for F+W Media's Krause Publications).

Some of our customers wanted to buy just the patterns from the kits because they already had the beads, so I also started self-publishing the patterns in book form. The first book sold well, so I expanded and did a number of them on different beading subjects. Acquisitions editor Tonia Davenport saw one of my self-published bracelet books and asked me to submit a proposal for a book on bead-woven bracelets for beginner to intermediate beaders. I'm pleased to say this book is the result of that request.

The idea behind this book is to teach you a specific stitch via a simple project. Bracelets make excellent projects for teaching and learning stitches—earrings are too small to really sink your teeth into, and a necklace is a much larger commitment and can be quite intimidating at times. Most of these bracelets can be completed fairly quickly, and you should be comfortable with the stitch by the time you complete the bracelet.

Each pattern (except the *Sampler Bracelet*) includes variations to the pattern using different beads, different sizes of beads, alternate ways to embellish or slight alterations in the pattern. The idea is to get you thinking about ways you can change a pattern to make it your own. That's how I ended up being a designer and author—I was forever changing patterns to make them mine.

I hope you can use this book as a starting-off place for "making it your own."

Getting Started

The materials used in this book are pretty basic—seed beads, thread and needles. Depending on the kind of beading you've been doing, you probably already have a stash that includes some of the various beads and threads called for in the projects. Of course you can practice with what you have on hand, or you may want to go out and buy some special beads. I could have done this entire book (with the exception of one project) with what I had on hand, but where's the fun in that? Trips to buy beads are as much fun as the actual beading. I also find that it is much easier to choose colors at the bead store. (I confess—I am a bead hoarder and have way more beads than I can ever use.) The store at which I was buying when I was planning projects for this book has limited stock, and that's OK. At times, having too many choices can become overwhelming, especially for a less experienced beader.

This book is intended to be a beginner to intermediate guide to a variety of weaves and stitches, and it uses a bracelet format to teach you those weaves and stitches. The projects all end with a button and loop closure or purchased finding. There are lots of different ways to make closures, but since the focus here is the stitch, I wanted to concentrate on that and not on making fancy closures.

The tips and techniques in this chapter only represent how I make and finish jewelry; they are by no means the only ways to do so. If you prefer a different method, by all means, go ahead and use it. There are no hard and fast rules in beading—each person is free to (and should!) put her individual stamp on her work.

Enjoy!

Most of the beads used in the following projects would be classified as seed beads. I also use drop beads, cube beads, peanut beads, Tila beads, hex beads, Delica beads, bicone crystals, fire polish beads, Chinese crystal rondelles, pressed glass beads and a few lamp-worked beads.

One thing to keep in mind at all times is that you should buy at least a few more beads than you think you will need, as you may need to adjust length; most of the time the instructions in this book will be for a 7" (18cm) bracelet. Another good reason to buy extra is that glass seed beads are manufactured in lots and often there is a slight color variation from one lot to another. Be sure all your beads are from the same lot.

Beads are usually described and sold by measurements in millimeters. The crystals, cubes and fire polish beads will be measured in millimeters. If there are two measurements, the hole length is usually given first. For example, a bead measuring 7mm × 5mm will have a hole that is 7mm long and a width of 5mm.

The exception to the millimeter rule is seed beads. A seed bead will be numbered with a "/0" or a "°" behind a number (6/0, 8/0, 11/0, 15/0 or larger; 6°, 8°, 11°, 15° or larger). The "°" stands for "ought" and comes from an old way of numbering seed beads. Remember that the larger the number, the smaller the bead.

The two major types of seed beads for weaving are Japanese and Czech. The seed beads used in this book are all Japanese. I prefer them because they have larger holes. That becomes very important as you weave back and forth through them many times. I suggest you avoid seed beads other than Japanese and Czech, as sizing is unlikely to be uniform.

Mention will be made throughout the book about starting your project with a "waste" or "stop" bead. This is a seed bead—usually not a color you are using in your design—that is tied on your thread with a single overhand knot to "stop" the beads you are stringing from falling off the end of your thread. At some point the bead will be removed (hence, the simple knot) so that you can use the tail to add a clasp or work it into your beading.

Seed Beads

The four sizes of seed beads used in the book are 6/0 (gold), 8/0 (chartreuse), 11/0 (pink), and 15/0 (teal). The smallest beads may also be referred to as 14/0. One or more of these beads are used in most of the projects in this book. They are usually purchased in tubes (Japanese) or on hanks (Czech).

Drop Beads

A drop bead has a hole which is offset to one side. It is often used on the end of a fringe strand to make a smooth end. Three kinds of drop beads were used in the book—3.4mm or 4mm drops and raindrops. The 3.4mm and 4mm drops are Japanese and the raindrops are an 8/0 size Czech bead with an off-center hole.

Cube Beads

Cube beads look just like their name implies—like cubes. They are six-sided (like dice) and come in a variety of sizes, including 1.5mm, 1.8mm, 3mm and 4mm.

Peanut Beads

Peanut beads get their name from their shape, as they are shaped just like peanuts. They are 2mm × 4mm and the hole is in the middle. They are fairly new on the market and a lot of fun to play with.

Tila Beads

Tila beads are two-hole square beads. They are very new on the market. The two holes allow the inventive beader to do some very unusual weaves.

Hex Beads

Hex beads are six-sided tubes, just as their name implies. They also come in a variety of sizes.

Delica Beads

Delicas are very regular tube-shaped Japanese seed beads. They are used a lot in loom work and peyote work. They come in 10/0 and 11/0 sizes. The ones used in this book are 10/0.

Crystal Beads

The crystals used in the book are all bicones. A bicone is a bead that is pointed on both ends, like a 3-D diamond. They are measured in millimeters. Most crystals are made by Swarovski, though there are a number of very fine and less expensive Czech alternatives. The ones used in this book measure 4mm and 6mm.

Fire Polish Beads

Fire polish beads are more reasonably priced faceted beads, usually Czech. They are sized in millimeters and come in a huge range of colors and sizes. The ones most commonly used in this book are 4mm and 6mm rounds.

Chinese Crystal Beads

These crystal beads are made in China. They are called rondelles because the bead is wider than the hole is long. Many have iridescent coatings. They are very sparkly and much less expensive than their European counterparts.

Pressed Glass Beads

Pressed glass beads are made in molds, so they are very uniform in shape and size. Pressed glass beads come in all sorts of shapes, sizes and colors of glass.

Buttons

Though not beads, I include buttons here, as they don't fit in with findings but they are used in a number of the projects in this book. A vintage button can make a much nicer looking clasp than a purchased finding.

As with beads, it is always a good idea to have a number of findings on hand. You may wish to start out with base metal instead of silver or gold, but that is up to you.

Because this book is limited to bracelets, you will only need a few basic findings. (For information on crimp beads, see page 13.)

Frequently Used Findings

Bead Cones or Tips

Decorative bead tips are used to hide the ends of strands, as in the *Sampler Bracelet*. They come in a variety of sizes depending on how many strand ends you need to cover.

Clamshells

The ones used in this book are the bottom-hole clamshell tips that close around your knot to hide it from view. They have a bar that you work around and into a loop to attach to the clasp.

Clasps

The most commonly used clasps are toggles and lobster claws, though there are lots of other types available. An assortment is shown here just to illustrate the variety you can find.

Eye Pins

You can thread beads on eye pins, use them to attach things to each other or to attach strands to a clasp, as in the *Sampler Bracelet*. A minimum length of 2" (5cm) is recommended.

Jump Rings

Jump rings are round or oval rings used to join two items together. They are used frequently to attach clasps.

Split Rings

Split rings are jump rings on steroids. They look more like springs; the benefit to using them is that they will not pull apart and come off your piece as jump rings sometimes can.

Beading Needles

For most beading in this book, a size 10 or 12 beading needle will work. Have plenty on hand as they bend easily.

Braided Filament

Most of the projects in this book are made with a braided filament line, like FireLine fishing line, WildFire or DandyLine, which are made for beading. FireLine is measured by weight in pounds, like 4lb, 6lb, 10lb, etc., and the bigger the number, the thicker the thread. A variety of sizes are used throughout this book, depending on the strength required. Both black and white lines are used as well. Be sure to use white line with clear crystals or other light-colored beads.

Silamide

Silamide is a twisted nylon tailoring thread with a waxy feel that is widely used in bead weaving. It is very good for peyote and square stitch weaving, and it comes in a variety of colors.

Nymo

Nymo is a nylon beading thread that comes on a small spool. Nymo stretches, so before you use it, cut off the length you will need and stretch it well before threading your needle. The greatest benefit of Nymo is that it comes in a large variety of colors.

Monofilament Fishing Line

Mono is a clear line that comes on a spool and is rated by weight. I rarely use mono line for beading, but occasionally it comes in handy, like in the *Bumples Bracelet*, which requires a very heavy stringing material to help the bumples maintain their shape.

I seldom use glue because I might want to go back through the beads at some point, and that is impossible if the holes are filled with glue. If you wish to use glue to be sure your threads are held securely, these are the glues used most often in the book. Other brands may be substituted, but if a specific kind of glue is called for, like fabric glue, be sure to use that kind of glue for best results.

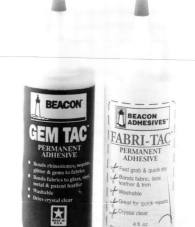

Fabri-Tac

Fabri-Tac is most often used to attach leather to leather or fabric.

Gem-Tac

Gem-Tac is used for attaching stones and metal pieces to leather and other surfaces.

Super Glue

Super Glue (not shown) is used to attach metal pieces together.

The following is a list of tools that you'll need to have on hand for the projects in this book.

Chain-Nose Pliers

Chain-nose pliers are pointed, smooth, flat-jawed pliers.

Bead Gauge

A bead gauge is a sliding ruler that allows you to accurately measure the size of beads in inches and millimeters. It takes all the guesswork out of sizing.

Crimp Pliers

Crimp pliers are for attaching and smoothing crimp beads.

Needle-Nose Pliers

Needle-nose pliers have a very pointed nose and are smooth-jawed.

Bead Sorting Dish

You will want to use something to prevent your beads from flying all over the place. Some beaders prefer a bead sorting dish—a small dish with separate compartments for each color or style of bead. Ceramic is best because plastic can have hold much static electricity. Other beaders prefer a beading mat, like a 9" × 12" (23cm × 30cm) piece of Vellux or leather.

Round-Nose Pliers

Round-nose pliers have round, pointed noses.

Split-Ring Pliers

These pliers handily open the split ring so it can be attached to your work.

Scissors

You will need two kinds of scissors—one for cutting thread and one for cutting braided filament (also known as blade scissors).

Wire Cutters

You'll need a pair of wire cutters for cutting stringing wire and head/eye pins.

Tool or Storage Box

You will want one centralized, organized place to keep all your materials and tools.

Tying knots is a pain, but sooner or later you are going to have to do it. Knots do make your work weaker, so I usually try to start out with a really long piece of thread—sometimes as much as two yards. If you don't want to deal with that much thread, then you will have to tie some knots as you work.

Some knots, however, are easier to do and work better than other knots. My favorite is a weaver's knot. If you get proficient at using this knot, you can change threads in the middle of a project without it being noticeable.

Weaver's Knot

A weaver's knot is a very effective way to join two threads together in the middle of a project.

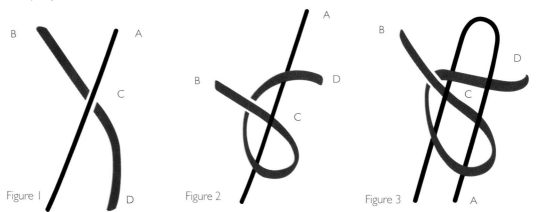

Figure 1　Figure 2　Figure 3

1 Referring to Figure 1, A is the end of the old thread and B is the end of the new thread. Cross them and hold them between your thumb and forefinger at point C. D is the new thread.

2 Pass D around and over A, up under B, and over A again, as shown in Figure 2.

3 Then turn A down over D, over the new thread B, and through the loop made by D, as shown in Figure 3.

4 Bring end B down and hold it with end A. Pull D tight, making sure you have pulled A down to where you want the knot. This knot slips through most seed beads and holds very well without being glued.

5 When you have tied on the new thread, weave the old end back through the work, being sure to tie an overhand knot after a few beads.

Half Hitch Knot

Half hitch knots are most often used to weave in thread ends.

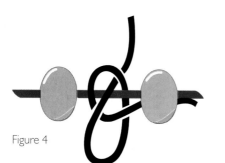

Figure 4

1 Take a small stitch over a thread between two beads in your work and pull the thread through until you have just a small loop of thread left.

2 Pass the needle through the loop, as shown in Figure 4, and pull tight.

3 Pass through a few beads and tie another knot.

4 Apply a very small amount of glue to the thread close to the knot and pass through a few more beads.

5 Pull the thread tightly and cut off the excess thread close to a bead.

Square Knot

A square knot is a good knot for ending threads and can also be used to change threads in the middle of a piece.

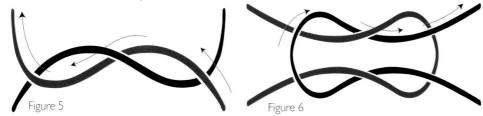

Figure 5   Figure 6

1 Cross the thread in your right hand over the thread in your left hand, around, and through to tie the knot, as shown in Figure 5.

2 Take the thread that's now in your left hand over the thread in your right hand, around, and through to tie another knot, as shown in Figure 6.

3 Put a small amount of glue on the knot to make sure it stays secure.

There are all sorts of ways to put a clasp on your bracelet. I find that the following methods work well for me.

Using a Button as a Clasp

1 Make the closure an integral part of your beaded piece by attaching a large bead or button at one end of the bracelet.

2 Bead a loop big enough to go over the bead or button on the other end. Many of the bracelets in the book include the button in the weave.

My Favorite Clamshell Method for Attaching Clasps

Crimp beads are usually used when you are working with stringing wire. I also use them inside the clamshell bead tips as support for tying off the threads. I'm not particularly good at tying nice-looking knots, so this is a method that works well for me.

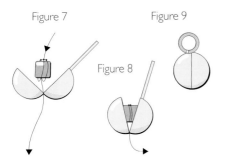

Figure 7   Figure 9

Figure 8

1 Pass the thread through a crimp bead and tie several square knots around the crimp bead.

2 Take the thread through the bottom hole of a clamshell bead tip, as shown in Figure 7, to begin the bracelet.

3 Glue the knots, trim the threads and close the clamshell around the crimp bead, as shown in Figure 8.

4 Bend the bar of the clamshell tip around in a loop, as shown in Figure 9.

The Direct Method

Attach the clasp directly to the bracelet with a few beads, or sew the clasp directly to the end of the band. Examples are shown in the project and variation photos.

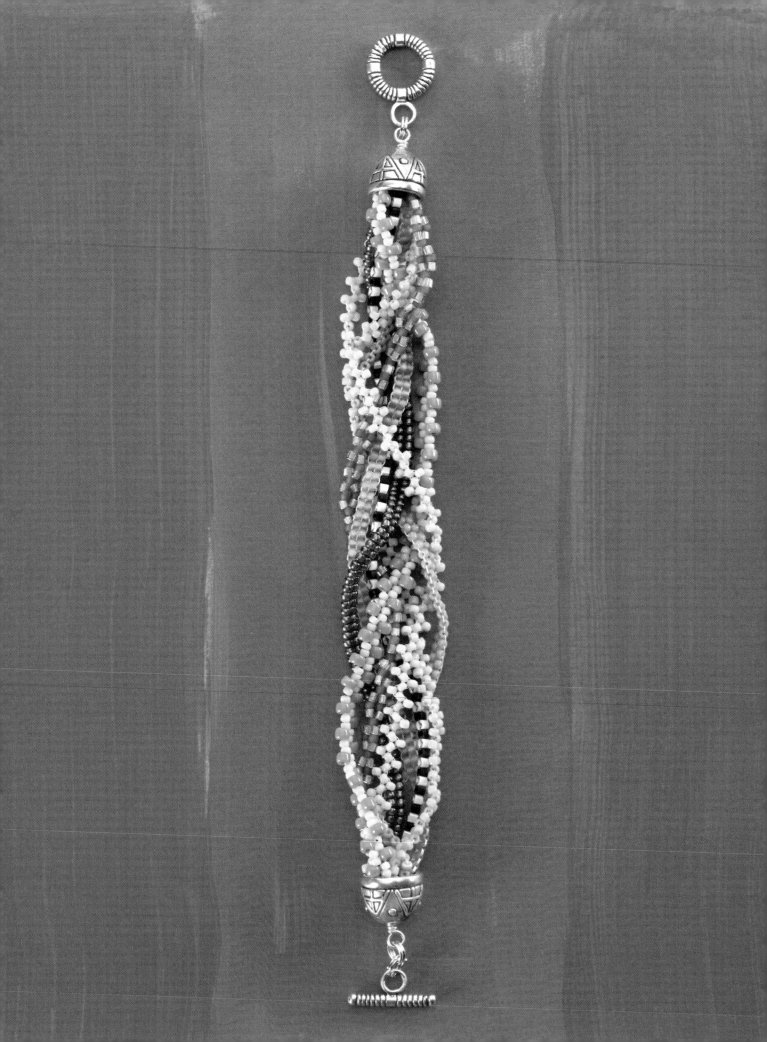

Chapter 1:

The Sampler Bracelet

The *Sampler Bracelet* is made up of eight bead-woven strands. Each strand is woven in a different color so it's easily identifiable; you can choose whatever colors you wish to use.

Since each strand is a very basic use of the weave, they are not very wide, just one to three beads each. If you made them much wider, the bracelet would be too bulky. Three kinds of beads are used in the sample: size 11/0 seed beads, size 8/0 seed beads and 1.5mm or 1.8mm cubes. For thread, you can use Silamide, Nymo or braided filament.

This is the only bracelet in the book that uses eye pins. After the strands are woven, they are tied to the eye of an eye pin. The pin is threaded through a decorative bead cap and attached to split rings. Finishing processes are covered in the instructions.

To know how long you will need to weave each strand, measure your wrist and subtract 1¼" to 1½" (3cm to 4cm) to allow for the clasp. The strands in the sample were woven 6¼" (16cm) long, and the finished bracelet measures about 7½" (19cm) long.

Grab some beads and let's get started.

MATERIALS FOR A 7½" (19CM) BRACELET

4lb or 6lb FireLine fishing line, .006" (.15mm) diameter Wild-Fire stringing thread, or Silamide or Nymo thread to match beads

Size 11/0 seed beads—7 colors

Size 8/0 seed beads—1 color

Size 1.5mm or 1.8mm cube beads—3 colors

2" (5cm) silver eye pins—2

Silver bell caps with a 10mm hole—2

10mm silver toggle clasp—1

4mm silver split rings—3

TOOLS

Size 10 or 12 beading needles—2

Scissors

Round-nose pliers

Chain-nose pliers

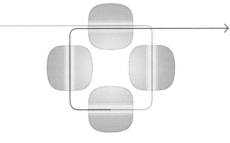

The Right-Angle Weave Strand (Two Needle Method)

1 Cut a yard (.9m) of thread and place a needle on each end. Be sure to keep the threads even in length.

2 Using size 11/0 seed beads, string four beads on one needle and center them on the thread.

3 Pass the second needle through the last bead you picked up, passing from the opposite direction, and pull up snug to form a diamond or square shape centered on the thread (Figure 1).

Figure 1

4 To continue, pick up two beads on the gray needle and one bead on the black needle. Then pass the black needle through the last bead on the gray needle and pull up snug, creating two squares (Figure 2). The threads are shown in two colors to make the illustrations and directions easier to follow.

5 Continue in this manner until you reach the desired length. You are continuously doing a figure eight with the two needles. Leave the thread tails hanging and set aside.

The Right-Angle Weave Strand (One Needle Method)

1 Cut a yard (.9m) of thread and single thread your needle.

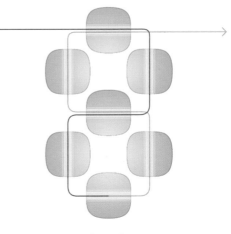

Figure 2

2 Using size 11/0 beads, pick up four beads and tie them together in a square knot between the first and fourth beads, 6" (15cm) from the end of the thread. Be sure to leave a little wiggle room.

3 Pass the needle and thread back through the first three beads, as shown (Figure 3).

4 String on beads three more beads (Figure 3).

5 Pass back through the third bead in the first square and then through the fifth and sixth beads in the second square (Figure 3).

6 Continue in this manner until you reach the length you need. Leave the thread tails hanging and set aside.

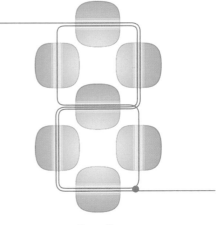

Figure 3

The Peyote Stitch Strand

1 Single thread your needle with a yard of thread.

2 Tie a waste bead within 6" (15cm) of the end of the thread.

3 Thread on three size 11/0 beads (Figure 4).

4 Pass your needle back through the first bead you picked up (Figure 4) and pull up snug so the third bead sits on the second bead.

5 Pick up a fourth bead and pass back through the third bead (Figure 5). Your beads should be sitting on each other in an offset pattern.

6 Pick up a fifth bead and pass back through the fourth bead (Figure 6).

7 Pick up a sixth bead and pass back through the fifth bead (Figure 6). Continue until you have the length you need.

8 Remove the waste bead. Leave the thread tails hanging and set aside.

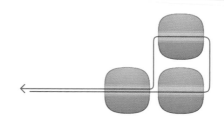

Figure 4

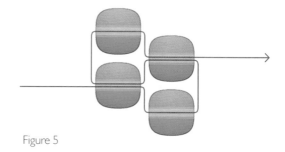

Figure 5

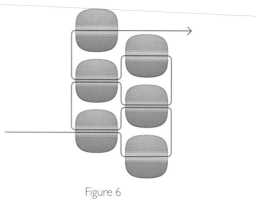

Figure 6

The Square Stitch Strand

1 Single thread your needle with about 4' (1.2m) of thread.

2 Tie a waste bead within 6" (15cm) of the end of the thread.

3 Pick up three size 11/0 beads and push them down the thread snug against the waste bead (Figure 7).

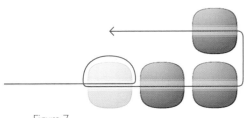

Figure 7

4 Pass the thread back through the second bead and then back up through the third bead (Figure 8).

5 Pick up a fourth bead and pass back through the first bead and then up through the fourth bead again (Figure 9).

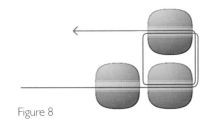

Figure 8

6 At this point, your thread is coming out of the second bead of the second row. Pass the needle and thread back through the first row and up and through the second row so you come out in the bead you started from. This is to align the rows and keep them straight. Do it after you add each new row.

7 Pick up a fifth bead (Figure 10). Pass back through the fourth bead, up through the fifth bead and continue weaving until you get the length you need.

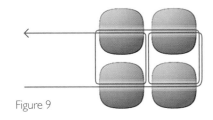

Figure 9

8 Remove the waste bead. Leave the thread tails hanging and set aside.

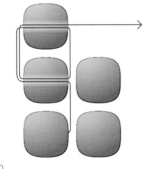

Figure 10

The Triangle Weave Strand

1 Single thread your needle with about 1 yard (.9m) of thread.

2 Pick up three size 11/0 beads. Take them to within 6" (15cm) of the end of your thread. Pass back through the first two beads you picked up, making a loop (Figure 11).

3 Pick up two more beads and pass back through the third bead from the first pass and the first bead of the last two you picked up, making a second loop offset from the first (Figure 12).

4 Pick up two more beads and pass back through the fifth and sixth beads (Figure 13). Each time you pick up two beads, you will pass back through a bead from the previous pattern.

5 Continue weaving in this manner until you have the length you need. Leave the thread tails hanging and set aside.

Figure 11

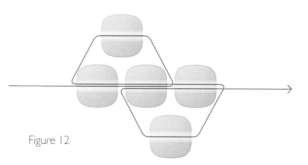

Figure 12

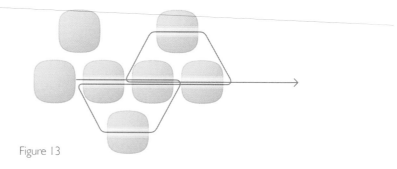

Figure 13

The Alternating Brick Stitch Strand

1 Single thread your needle with about 1 yard (.9m) of thread.

2 Pick up two size 11/0 seed beads and one size 8/0 seed bead. Pass through the two size 11/0 beads again, forming a circle (Figure 14). Push the circle down the thread so you have a 6" (15cm) tail. Your working thread and tail should be coming out both sides of the size 11/0 beads.

3 Pick up one size 8/0 bead and two size 11/0 beads.

4 Coming from the back and working towards the front, pass your needle under the thread between the size 8/0 beads and two size 11/0 beads from the first row (Figure 15). You will be looping around the thread from the previous pattern.

5 Pass the needle up through the newly added size 11/0 beads (Figure 16).

6 Continue repeating steps 3 through 5 until you have the length you need. Leave the thread tails hanging and set aside.

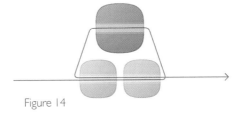

Figure 14

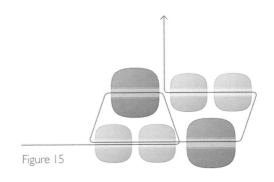

Figure 15

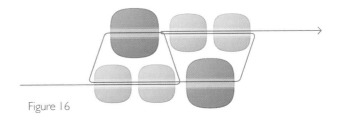

Figure 16

The Netting Stitch Strand

1 Single thread your needle with 18" (46cm) of thread.

2 Tie on a pink waste bead 6" (15cm) from the end of the thread.

3 Begin stringing, alternating one pink size 11/0 bead with one pink cube bead until you get slightly more than the length you need. End with a pink seed bead. Tie on another pink waste bead. Remove the needle.

4 Re-thread your needle with another 18" (46cm) of thread.

5 Pass the needle and thread through the waste bead on one end of the bracelet and tie off, leaving a 6" (15cm) tail.

6 Pass through the first pink size 11/0 bead and thread on one cube, one size 11/0 bead and one cube (Figure 17).

7 Not counting the waste bead, pass the needle through the third pink 11/0 bead in the first row.

8 Repeat step 6 and pass through the fifth size 11/0 bead in the first row.

9 Continue in this manner adding the cube–11/0 seed bead–cube pattern and passing through every other 11/0 pink bead in the first strand until you reach the other end of the strands. Check for length and add or subtract as you need for the length you want.

10 Tie off the thread using the waste bead on the other end. Leave the thread tails hanging and set aside.

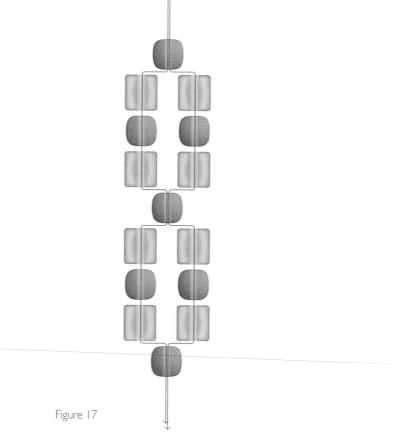

Figure 17

The Herringbone (Ndebele) Weave Strand

1 Single thread your needle with about 1 yard (.9m) of thread.

2 Leaving a 6" (15cm) tail, pick up four size 11/0 beads and pass back through them so two sit atop two (Figure 18).

3 Your working thread should be coming out of the lower right bead. Pass left into the lower left bead then across the center and out through the upper right bead (Figure 19). You have just made the ladder stitch base often used to start the herringbone weave.

4 Your working thread should be coming out of the upper right bead (Figure 19). Pick up two new beads.

5 Pass the thread down through the upper left bead of the first four you picked up, across the center, and up through the first bead you picked up in step 4 (Figure 20). Pull snugly. The new beads should sit at a very slight angle to each other.

6 Repeat steps 4 and 5 until you have the length you need (Figure 21). Leave the thread tails hanging and set aside.

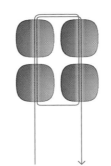

Figure 18

Figure 19

Figure 20

Figure 21

The Ladder Stitch Strand
(Two Needle Method)

1 Place a needle on each end of 1 yard (.9m) of thread.

2 Pick up one black cube and one white cube on the black needle and center them on the thread (Figure 22). The threads are shown in two colors to make the illustrations and directions easier to follow.

3 Pass the red needle through the white cube from the opposite direction and pull snug so the beads sit side by side.

4 Pick up a black cube on one needle and pass the red needle through it from the opposite direction.

5 Continue in this manner, alternating black and white beads, until you have the length you need.

6 Remove the needles. Leave the thread tails hanging and set aside.

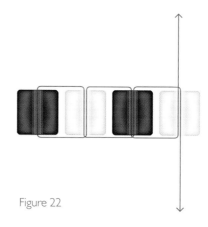

Figure 22

The Ladder Stitch Strand
(One Needle Method)

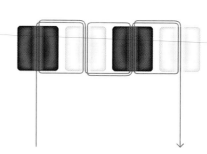

1 Single thread the needle with 1 yard (.9m) of thread.

2 Pick up one black and one white cube. Pass the needle back through both beads in a circular manner (Figure 23). Pull beads up so they sit side by side.

3 Pick up one black bead. Pass back through the white cube and the black one you just picked up (Figure 23).

4 Repeat step 3, but this time add a white cube.

5 Continue in this manner until you have the length you need. Remove the needle. Leave the thread tails hanging and set aside.

Figure 23

Finishing the Bracelet

1 Trim thread ends on all strands to 6" (15cm). If some of the strands that don't have thread hanging from the end, slip additional thread through the end bead, leave it doubled and trim to 6" (15cm).

2 Using the round-nose pliers, slip the eye of one eye pin down one pliers jaw until it is snug. Close the pliers and bend the pin around the eye once so you double the eye. You may need to reposition the pliers. Repeat for the other pin.

3 Begin tying one end of each strand to the eye of one pin (a couple of double knots should do the trick). Trim the thread ends and place a drop of glue on the knots, if you like. Allow the glue to dry.

4 Repeat step 3 for the other end of the strands.

5 Slip a bell cap over one pin, covering the ends of the strands and the knots.

6 Hold the pin tight against the top of the bell cap with chain-nose pliers, and bend the pin to a right angle (Figure 24).

7 Switch to round-nose pliers and grab either side of the bend (Figure 25); roll the pin around the pliers, making a loop.

8 Wrap the remainder of the pin around the pin shaft, below the loop (Figure 26). Trim the excess wire.

9 Repeat steps 5 through 8 for the other end of the bracelet.

10 Attach the loop end of the toggle to one wrapped eye pin with one split ring.

11 Attach the bar end of the toggle to the other end using two split rings.

Figure 24

Figure 25

Figure 26

Chapter 2:

Right-Angle Weave

Without a doubt, my favorite stitch is the right-angle weave. When I learned the stitch, it was called double needle right-angle weave, but lately I've seen a lot of references to it also being called cross weave. Whatever you call it, the stitch is extremely versatile and a good one to have in your beading repertoire. The projects in this chapter are done in the double needle method, which I prefer (instructions for both the one and two needle methods can be found in *Chapter 1: The Sampler Bracelet*, page 17). All of the projects can be done with a single needle; they will just take longer to complete.

Autumn Leaves Bracelet

There are countless beads out there that will work with right-angle weave. The weave seems to work best if you can choose beads that are uniform in shape and size, and while the examples shown all use different sizes and shapes of beads, each bead is uniform since these beads are all pressed glass. Many shapes of Czech and Japanese glass beads work really well. Some gemstone beads will work if they are well matched, but often the cheaper ones have too many irregularly shaped beads. That can be interesting in some contexts but annoying if you are looking for uniformity of pattern.

The beads in the *Autumn Leaves Bracelet* came in the variegated colors you see. I used them randomly as they came off the strands. The bronze fire polish and the matte olive green seed beads blend nicely with the various colors in the leaf beads.

Variations

Orange & Bronze Right-Angle Weave Beaded Bracelet

The orange and bronze crystals bracelet was made in exactly the same manner as the *Autumn Leaves Bracelet* except the side patterns consist of one seed bead, one crystal and one seed bead. In traditional right-angle weave, the patterns are square (or diamond shaped, depending on the beads). You can have as many beads on a side as you want as long as the sides are consistent.

Pink & Brown Right-Angle Weave Beaded Bracelet

The pink and brown bracelet uses an unusual diamond-shaped bead which was too large to use in every pattern, so it was alternated with a round bead. This creates a zigzag pattern of round beads down the center of the band. The varieties of beads to use and the patterns you can make are endless with right-angle weave.

MATERIALS FOR AN 8" (20cm) BRACELET

14lb FireLine fishing line—1 to 2 yards (1m to 2m)

2mm crimp beads—2

Gold clamshell bead tips—2

Size 11/0 olive green matte seed beads—96

6mm bronze fire polish beads—22

4mm × 12mm variegated autumn colors Czech glass leaf beads—42

15mm gold toggle clasp—1

TOOLS

Scissors

Size 10 beading needles—2

Round-nose pliers

Chain-nose pliers

Starting the Bracelet

1 Cut about 4' (1.2m) of fishing line and place a needle on each end. Pull the thread ends so they are even.

2 Pick up one crimp bead on one needle and center it on the thread.

3 Pass the needle through the bead a couple of times.

4 Pass both needles through a clamshell bead tip from the inside out. Close the clamshell around the crimp bead.

5 Use round-nose pliers to bend the bar of the clamshell around the bar end of the clasp now, as shown in Figure 1, or you can wait until you have finished the beading.

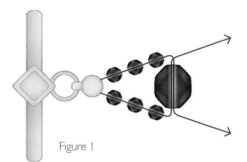

Figure 1

Beading the Bracelet

1 On each needle, pick up three green seed beads. Refer to Figure 1.

2 Pick up one 6mm bead on one needle and pass the second needle through it from the opposite direction, as shown in Figure 1. Pull the threads tight.

3 On each needle, pick up one seed bead, one leaf and one seed bead.

4 On one needle, pick up a 6mm bead. Pass the second needle through the bead from the opposite direction and pull snug on the threads (Figure 2).

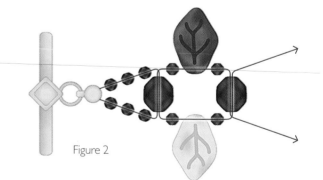

Figure 2

5 Repeat steps 3 and 4 one more time, as shown in Figure 3.

6 Continue down the bracelet repeating steps 3 and 4 until you have the length you need. Usually you'll need to allow 1" to 1½" (1cm to 3cm) for the clasp.

7 Finish your beaded section when you exit either side of a 6mm bead.

Finishing the Bracelet

1 Pick up three seed beads on each needle, as shown in Figure 4.

2 Pass both needles through a clamshell bead tip from the bottom up.

3 Pick up a crimp bead on one needle. Tie off the threads against the crimp bead. Pass one needle through the crimp bead again and tie off once more.

4 Cut the thread ends and close the crimp bead with chain-nose pliers.

5 Using round-nose pliers, bend the bar of the clamshell around the attaching loop on the loop end of the toggle, as shown in Figure 4.

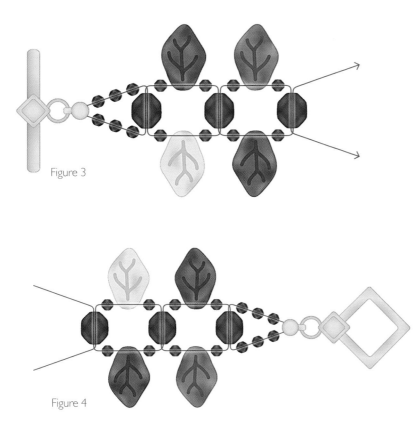

Figure 3

Figure 4

Beaded Bead Bracelet

One of my favorite things to do with right-angle weave is make beaded beads. The two beads in this bracelet are about the easiest beaded beads you can make. You can use either a one or two needle method to make them; do whichever is easiest for you. Instructions for both methods are given in *Chapter 1: The Sampler Bracelet*. The following instructions are given in the two needle method but would be easy to adapt.

This bracelet consists of four small beaded beads and three larger beaded barrel beads strung on wire with fire polish beads and seed beads in between. The size of the bracelet can be adjusted depending on how many of each bead you choose to use.

You will pass your needle through the base beads many times. This helps strengthen the bead to keep it from collapsing.

Variation

6mm Turquoise Beaded Bead Bracelet

This bracelet only uses three beaded beads because each was made with 6mm fire polish beads instead of the 4mm beads. Using larger beads makes the beaded beads bigger. The crosses were made with size 11/0 seed beads. You can use a variety of beads to make the beaded beads. They are especially nice when made with crystals.

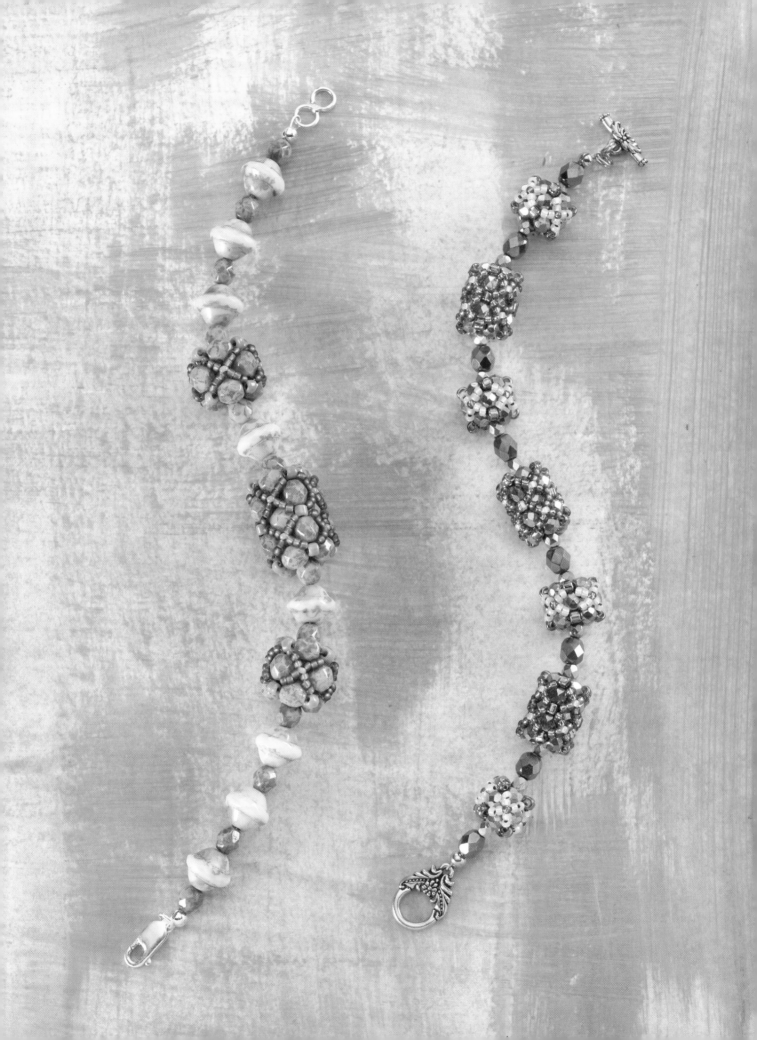

MATERIALS FOR A 7" (18cm) BRACELET

.008" (.2mm) diameter WildFire beading thread or 6lb or 8lb FireLine fishing line

.018" (.5mm) diameter Beadalon stringing wire—wrist measurement plus 3" (8cm)

4mm bronze fire polish beads—122

Size 11/0 yellow luster seed beads—2 grams

Size 11/0 purple silver-lined seed beads—2 grams

Size 8/0 green silver-lined seed beads—68

2mm gold crimp beads—2

Gold toggle clasp—1

Gold crimp covers—2

6mm bronze fire polish beads—8

4mm gold split rings—2

TOOLS

Scissors

Size 10 beading needles—2

Wire cutters

Crimping pliers

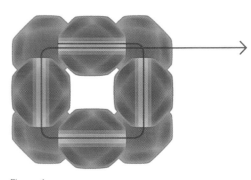

Figure 5

Making the Spacer Beads

1 Cut about 4' (1.2m) of beading thread or fishing line and place a needle on each end. Pull the thread ends so they are even.

2 Referring to the instructions for the basic right-angle weave in *Chapter 1: The Sampler Bracelet* (page 17), make a band of right-angle weave three patterns long using the 4mm bronze fire polish beads.

3 Pick up one fire polish bead on each needle. (Refer to Figure 5.)

4 Pass each through the point bead of the first pattern you made, from the opposite direction, as shown in Figure 5, rolling the beads around to form a cube. Pull snug. You have now completed the base of the bead.

5 Pass the threads back through all of the beads, following the pattern to reinforce.

6 One thread should be coming out of each side of the point bead. Pass one of these threads through the beads on the edge of the cube of beads, as shown in Figure 6, to tighten. Pass through the first bead a second time. Repeat for the other side.

Figure 6

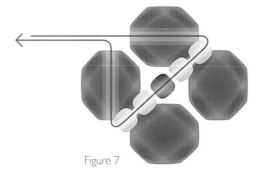

Figure 7

7 Using one thread only (ignore the other thread for the time being) and coming out of a top bead (Figure 6), pick up two yellow seed beads, one purple seed bead and two yellow seed beads. Pass diagonally across the square of larger beads and pass up and through the bead on the left side of the square (Figure 7). You may also do this left to right, if it works better for you.

8 Continue around the cube, repeating step 7 until you have come back to where you started.

9 At this point you will go back the other way (Figure 8). Pick up two yellow seed beads. Pass through the purple seed bead from the top down. Pick up two yellow seed beads. Pass up through the large side bead (Figure 8), and continue around the cube, repeating this step passing up or down through the purple bead, depending on the direction your needle is heading.

10 With the second needle, pass around the edge of the cube (above the X's of beads), picking up a size 8/0 (green) bead between each large bead. Pass through each a second time to reinforce (Figure 9). Repeat for the other side. Tie off the threads.

11 Repeat steps 1 through 10 three more times, making a total of four small spacer beads. Set the beads aside.

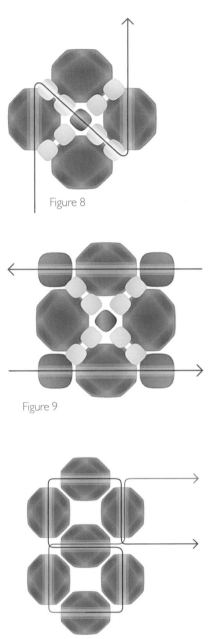

Figure 8

Figure 9

Making the Barrel Beads

1 To begin the barrel bead, using about 4' (1.2m) of thread, make two right-angle weave patterns with the 4mm fire polish beads (Figure 10), but on the second pattern, place the three beads on one needle and pass the second needle (shown in red) through the last of them so your threads will be coming out the side of the pattern and away from the beading.

2 To start the second row (Figure 11), pick up three of the 4mm beads on the needle pointing to the top (shown in red) and pass the second needle (shown in black) through the last bead and pull snug.

3 Pass the red needle down through the side bead of the first pattern, as shown in Figure 11, and pick up two beads.

4 Pass the black needle through the second bead and pull snug. The threads should point to the side (Figure 11).

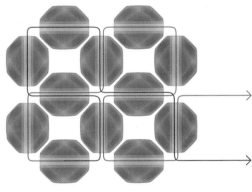

Figure 10

Figure 11

5 To make the third row, add two more patterns, as you did in the previous steps (Figure 12).

6 Bend the pattern around until you have a U shape. Pick up one bead on the top (red) needle, as shown in Figure 12. Pass down the side bead on the opposite side of the U.

7 Pick up another bead on the red needle and pass the black needle through it and pull snug, as shown in Figure 13.

8 To finish the pattern and join the beaded bead, pass each thread through a side bead, as shown in Figure 13. Pick up a bead on one needle, pass the other needle through it, and pull snug.

9 Pass one needle through the edge beads, as you did in Figure 5 (*Making the Small Spacer Beads*). Pass the second needle through the beading, being sure to follow the pattern around, and bring it out the other end. Pass the thread around again, as shown in Figure 5, to reinforce that end.

10 Using one thread, begin embellishing the sides of the bead, as you did in steps 7 through 9 of *Making the Small Spacer Beads*. This time use two purple seed beads, one yellow seed bead and two purple seed beads to make the crosses. Embellish one half of the bead, then pass the needle through the pattern of beads and embellish the second half. Each of the four sides of your finished piece should look like Figure 14.

11 Use the remaining needle. Pass through one of the corner beads, as shown in Figure 15, and pick up a green size 8/0 bead. Pass the needle through the next corner bead.

12 Pass the needle through an end bead and back through a corner bead, following the thread path indicated in Figure 15. Pick up a green bead and pass through the next corner bead.

13 Continue moving up and down the bead, adding a green bead in between two corner beads, until all four sides are done (Figure 15).

14 Pass around the top and bottom edges of the bead, adding a green size 8/0 bead between the fire polish beads, as shown in Figure 16.

15 Tie off the threads and trim the thread tails.

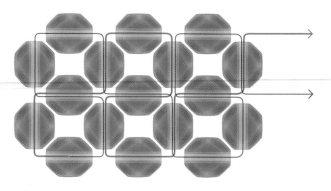

Figure 12

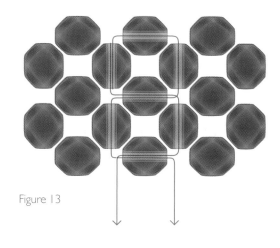

Figure 13

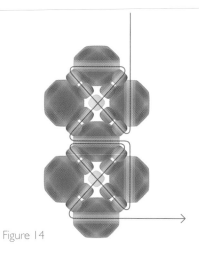

Figure 14

Assembling the
Bracelet

1 Thread one crimp bead on the end of the wire. Pass the wire through the small loop of the loop end of the toggle. Pass the wire back through the crimp. Leave a ½" (1cm) tail. Crimp using crimping pliers and following the manufacturer's directions. Cover with a crimp cover.

2 Begin threading on one 6mm fire polish bead, one 4mm fire polish bead and one spacer bead. Because the spacer bead has a big hole, you may want to thread on enough seed beads to fill the hole; they should easily fit inside the spacer.

3 Next, add one 4mm, one 6mm, one 4mm and a barrel bead. Again, thread on enough seed beads to fill the barrel bead.

4 Alternate the 4mm/6mm/4mm sequence with a barrel and a spacer as shown in the photo on page 33.

5 End with one 4mm and one 6mm.

6 Insert one split ring into the other split ring and attach one to the bar end of the toggle.

7 Pass the wire through a crimp bead and the end split ring. Pass the wire back through the crimp. Pull the wire snugly so the beads have just a little play and there's enough room for the crimp cover.

8 Smash the crimp and cover with a crimp cover. Trim the wire ends.

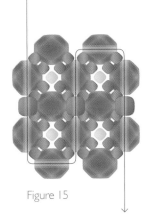

Figure 15

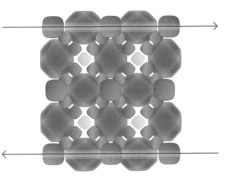

Figure 16

Bumples Bracelet

I included this bracelet in the chapter on right-angle weave because it is done with two threads but an uneven number of beads. Each pattern in the bumple is a pentagon using five beads per pattern. The bumps are actually half of a dodeca-hedron sphere. Each bump is comprised of six patterns (five sides and the top). The bumples are made using 30lb monofilament fishing line. The heavy mono is necessary if the bumps are to maintain their shape.

I suggest you practice making a sample bumple using three colors of beads before you begin making the bracelet—it will be much easier to see and understand how the beads work together.

Variation

Black & Purple Bumples Bracelet

Chinese crystals come in a range of glittering colors. This bracelet would be great for that fancy night on the town.

MATERIALS FOR A 7½" (19cm) BRACELET

30lb monofilament line

6mm Chinese crystal rondelles—140

8mm Chinese crystal rondelles—20

8lb FireLine fishing line or .008" (.2mm) diameter WildFire beading thread

3mm drop beads—102

Silver magnetic clasp—1

TOOLS

Scissors

Size 10 beading needles—2

Note: The graphics are done in three colors to make it easier to understand bead placement while you make a sample bead. The beads will be referred to by these colors even though the bracelet is woven in just one color.

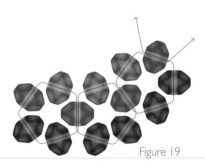

Figure 17

Making the Bumples

1 Cut about 4' (1.2m) of monofilament line (thread).

2 On one end of your thread, pick up one red, one blue, one red and two black 6mm beads (Figure 17).

3 Pass the other end of the thread through the first red bead you picked up. Center all the beads on the line and pull snug (Figure 17).

4 Hold the beads so the thread is coming out the side of the pattern (Figure 17).

5 Pick up two black beads on the bottom thread (Figure 18).

6 Pick up one blue and one red bead on the top thread (Figure 18).

7 Pass the bottom thread through the red bead and pull snug (Figure 18).

8 To make the third pattern, repeat steps 5 through 7 (Figure 19).

9 For the fourth pattern, repeat steps 5 through 7 (Figure 20).

10 To finish the bead by joining the ring, pick up one blue bead on the top thread (Figure 21).

11 Pass the thread back through all the blue beads with the same end of the thread as in step 10 (Figure 21), including the blue bead added in step 10.

12 When you have passed through all the blue beads, pass the thread through the red bead from the very first pattern (your thread should be pointing toward it (Figure 21).

13 When you are done, you should have a thread exiting the first and fifth red beads. Hold your project on the side so you are looking at the red/blue/red beads (Figure 22).

14 Pick up two black beads on the right-hand thread (Figure 22).

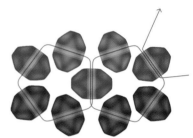

Figure 18

Figure 19

Figure 20

15 Pass the left-hand thread through the second black bead you picked up (Figure 22). Pull snug.

16 Pass one end of the thread through all the black beads and tie off securely with the other end of the thread. Trim the thread ends close to the knot. You have completed the practice bumple.

17 Make six bumples with the 6mm beads in the color of your choice.

18 Make one bumple with the 8mm beads.

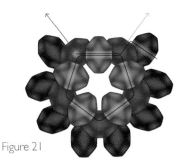

Figure 21

Adding the Drop Beads

1 Single thread your needle with 1 yard (.9m) of FireLine.

2 Tie the end of the FireLine around the mono, in a square knot in the bottom of one bumple.

3 As you look at the beaded piece, you will see three bead patterns where the pentagon shapes intersect. Pass the needle around the piece, adding a drop bead in the center of each three-bead pattern (Figure 23).

4 Pass the needle through the bottom beads until you get a three-bead pattern. Pick up a drop bead (Figure 23).

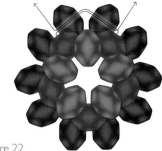

Figure 22

5 Pass through the next two black beads in the base of the bumple until you get to the next three-bead pattern, and pick up a drop bead (Figure 23).

6 Repeat step 5 three more times.

7 This time, instead of following around the base of the bumple, pass the needle up and to the right, to the next three-bead pattern, and add a drop bead.

8 Then pass around the bumple, adding a drop bead between each three-bead pattern until you are done.

9 Tie off the threads and clip the ends. Repeat for all remaining bumples.

Assembling the Bracelet

1 Cut 1 yard (.9m) of FireLine and place a needle on each end.

2 Attach one end of the magnetic clasp to the center of the thread. Pass through the clasp several times to reinforce.

3 Using one needle at a time, pick up one drop bead, two rondelles and one drop bead.

4 Pass the needle through three bottom beads of a 6mm bumple.

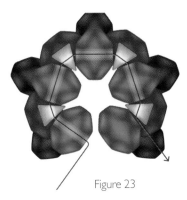

Figure 23

5 Pick up one drop bead, one rondelle and one drop bead on each needle and pass each through three beads on either side of the next 6mm bumple.

6 Repeat step 5.

7 Repeat step 5, but this time pick up the 8mm bumple.

8 Finish the second half of the bracelet similarly, but in reverse order with the 6mm bumples.

9 Attach the other half of the clasp. Tie off securely and trim the thread ends.

Chapter 3:

Peyote Stitch

Diagonal, twill and gourd are all names for the stitch that today is commonly called peyote. The term "peyote" was originally and still is used by Native Americans to describe beadwork done with this stitch for religious and ceremonial purposes. Currently, peyote is the most commonly used stitch in bead weaving. It is an excellent weave to use by itself and it combines well with a variety of other stitches. The beads in peyote stitch are offset like paving bricks. They are stacked on each other in columns vertically as you weave rows horizontally. Because the rows are offset by half of a bead, it is easier to count the rows on a diagonal. The projects in this chapter are meant to show the diversity of the stitch, but they don't begin to make a dent in the overall variety one can accomplish with peyote.

Spiral Rope Bracelet

The *Spiral Rope Bracelet* is done in a tubular peyote stitch. If you used all the same size beads, you would make a smooth tube. When you use different sizes of beads, you end up with an undulating spiral. The stitch is essentially done the same as flat peyote except that you are working in a circle. It is a little difficult to get the spiral started because the first few rows look like a muddle, but it eventually begins to take shape. Just keep in mind that after stringing on the base ring, you will always pick up a bead the same color as the bead you just exited.

And because you are working in a circle, you can weave both ends of the tube together and make a bangle bracelet. Personally, I am not a big fan of bangle bracelets, so this bracelet and the variation bracelets have clasps, and each is clasped in a different manner to give you some ideas for how to finish your project.

You can also vary the sizes of the beads and the number of beads you use; just remember that for each bead you want to use in the actual spiral, you have to use two of each in the base ring.

Variations

Turquoise Spiral Rope Bracelet

This bracelet is made the same way as the main project bracelet but uses three sizes of the same color bead. It is finished by passing the thread ends through a 6mm bead and into clamshell bead tips, at which point they are tied off. The clamshells are attached to a decorative box clasp.

Chartreuse Spiral Rope Bracelet

This bracelet uses size 11/0 and 8/0 seed beads and 4mm fire polish beads to make the spiral. A length of beading wire was inserted through the middle. Decorative end caps were placed over the ends of the wire and the tube. The wire was attached to the lobster claw clasp with crimp beads and crimp covers.

MATERIALS FOR AN 8" (20cm) BRACELET

.008" (.2mm) diameter WildFire beading thread or 8lb
FireLine fishing line

Size 11/0 brown matte seed beads—10 grams

Size 8/0 cream seed beads—10 grams

Size 6/0 gold luster seed beads—10 grams

Small gold lobster clasp—1

Fine gold-colored chain—8" (20cm)

Gold clasp tag—1

5mm gold split rings—2

TOOLS

Size 10 beading needle—1

Scissors

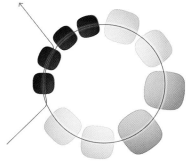

Figure 1

Figure 2

Making the Spiral Tube

1 Single thread your needle with about 4' (1.2m) of thread.

2 Refer to Figure 1, and thread on four brown, two cream, two
gold luster and two cream seed beads.

3 Pass through the first two brown seeds you picked up, making
a loop. Push the loop down the thread, leaving a 10" (25cm)
tail. You have made the first two rows of tubular peyote.

4 Start the third row by picking up one additional brown bead.
Skip the next (third) brown bead in the ring, as shown in Figure
2, and pass through the fourth brown bead in the base ring.
Because you exited a brown bead, you picked up a brown
bead. Keep the thread tension tight.

5 Pick up a brown bead. Skip the first cream bead in the base
ring and pass through the second cream bead, as shown in
Figure 3. Because you exited a brown bead, you picked up a
brown bead.

6 Pick up a cream bead. Skip the first gold luster bead in the base
ring and pass through the second gold luster bead, as shown
in Figure 4. Because you exited a cream bead, you picked up
a cream bead.

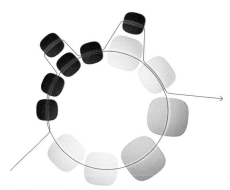

Figure 3

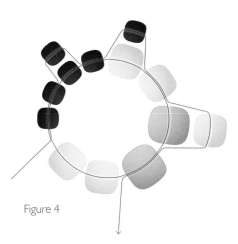

Figure 4

7 Pick up a gold luster bead. Skip the next cream bead in the base ring and pass through the following cream bead, as shown in Figure 5. Because you exited a gold bead, you picked up a gold bead.

8 Pick up a cream bead and pass through the brown bead you picked up in step 4. Refer to Figure 6. You have completed your third row.

9 Continue passing around the ring, making sure to pick up the same color of bead you just exited.

10 It will take several rounds for the pattern to emerge. You may wish to insert a pen into the beginning of the tube to give it definition until it begins to hold its shape on its own.

11 Continue adding beads until you reach the length you need for your bracelet.

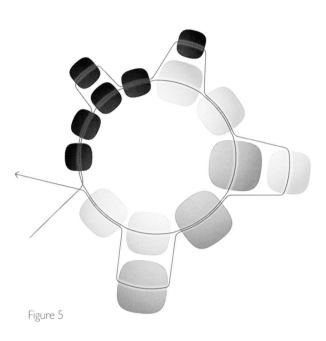

Figure 5

Finishing the Bracelet

1 Attach the lobster clasp to one end of the chain with a split ring.

2 Pass the other end of the chain through the beaded tube.

3 Attach the clasp tag to the other end of the chain with the second split ring.

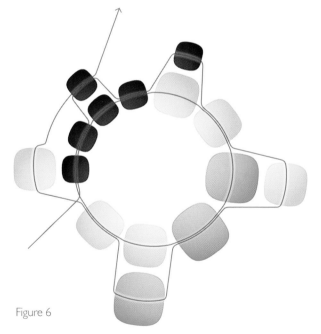

Figure 6

Embellished Peyote Bracelet

This bracelet is woven in a basic flat peyote stitch in an eight-bead band. The band is then embellished with peanut and seed beads. A whip stitch is added to the edge, which places the beads on their sides, covering the thread edge of the band. A simple button and loop closure finishes the band.

In this bracelet, as in the *Spiral Rope Bracelet* (page 44), you will be picking up the beads for the first two rows in your first pass. The ninth bead is the start of the third row. One important thing to remember with this bracelet is to keep your tension snug; you want the beads to sit next to each other with almost no room between them.

Variations

Turquoise & Purple Embellished Peyote Bracelet

This version features the same eight-bead band as the project bracelet, but it has two rows of turquoise size 10 Delica beads, one of white, two of purple, one of white and two of turquoise. It is edge-finished in the same manner as the project bracelet. The white rows are embellished by whip stitching a second white row on top of the first one. A three-strand bracelet clasp is attached in place of the button and loop closure.

Green Embellished Peyote Bracelet

This bracelet also has eight rows of beads—one matte green, one pale beige, four green iris, one pale beige and one matte green. The edge is embellished with loops of seed beads consisting of one matte, one beige, one green iris, one beige and one matte. The button loop is made by continuing a peyote stitch with the matte and beige beads off one side and weaving them into the other side. The loops go all around the edges of the bracelet, including the closure loop. A small shank button is sewn on the other end.

MATERIALS FOR A 7" (18cm) BRACELET

6lb crystal FireLine fishing line or .006" (.15mm) diameter Wildfire beading thread

Size 11/0 copper-lined translucent copper seed beads—6 grams

Size 11/0 copper-lined translucent white seed beads—10 grams

¾" (2cm) shank copper button—1

2mm x 4mm bronze peanut beads—2 grams

TOOLS

Size 10 or 12 beading needle—1

Scissors

Glue (optional)

Making the Basic Band

1 Single thread your needle with as much thread as you can handle.

2 Tie a waste bead about 8" (20cm) up from the end of the thread.

3 Begin by threading on two copper, four white, and three copper beads, as shown in Figure 7. These beads become rows 1 and 2 and the ninth bead becomes the first bead of the third row.

4 Pass the thread back through the seventh bead from the end, as shown in Figure 7, and pull the thread snug until the ninth bead sits atop the eighth bead, as shown.

5 Pick up one white bead and pass the needle through the fifth bead (white) in the first row, as shown in Figure 8.

6 Pick up another white bead and pass through the third bead in the first row, as shown in Figure 9.

7 For the final bead in the third row, pick up one copper bead and pass through the first bead in the first row, as shown in Figure 10.

8 At this point your beads should begin moving against each other and forming up and down beads, as shown in Figure 11. Keep in mind that in peyote, the rows are offset like paving bricks, and by the time you have completed the third row as you just did, this pattern should be visible. You may remove the waste bead and work the beginning tail into the work at this point, or it can wait until later.

9 To begin the fourth row, pick up a copper bead and pass the needle through the first "up" bead from the previous row, as shown in Figure 12. Continue across the row adding the correct color of bead each time.

10 Continue adding rows as you have done so far until you reach about ½" (1cm) short of the length you need to go around your wrist.

Figure 7

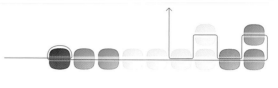

Figure 8

Figure 9

Figure 10

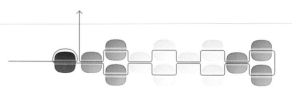

Figure 11

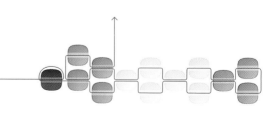

Figure 12

Adding the Closure

1 Sew the button to the top of the bracelet about ¼" (6mm) from the end of the band.

2 On the other end, bring a thread out of the end of the band and alternately add on two copper beads and one peanut until you get a loop long enough to pass around the button.

3 Tie off all threads securely.

Adding the Edging

1 Bring a thread out of one side of one end of the band, as shown in Figure 13.

2 Pass through a white bead and through the thread on the side of the band, as shown in Figure 13, making a loop around the thread.

3 Pick up another bead and repeat. You are whip stitching the new beads in place against the thread on the edge of the band and they should fall into place lying on their sides.

4 Repeat for both sides of the band.

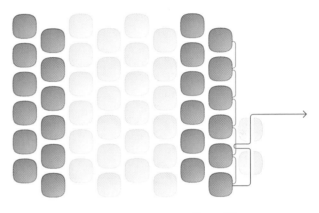

Figure 13

Adding the Embellishment

1 Begin at the loop end of the band and work a single thread into the beading, bringing the needle out between the fifth and sixth beads in the row (between two white beads).

2 Pick up one copper, one peanut and one copper bead and pass diagonally left across the band, passing the needle between the third and fourth beads (both white beads). Refer to Figure 14.

3 Pass the needle into the band again, working right, and repeat steps 1 and 2 down the length of the band.

4 Tie off the threads securely using half hitch knots and a drop of glue if you like.

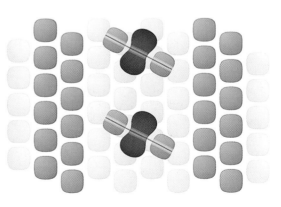

Figure 14

Scalloped Peyote with Fringe Bracelet

The *Scalloped Peyote With Fringe Bracelet* is done with exactly the same stitch as the **Embellished Peyote Bracelet** (page 48), but that's where the similarity ends. You need to forget what you learned making the embellished bracelet, where snug tension is very important. In this bracelet, the lack of tension is what makes the scallop. If you do this bracelet without the fringe, you will end up with something that looks like rickrack. The fringe tends to hide that some, but you should still be able to see the band undulating.

Unless you are very familiar with peyote stitch, it is probably a good idea to do this bracelet with size 8/0 seed beads and 4mm drop beads. The variation bracelet uses a Czech glass 8/0 seed bead with an off-center hole called a raindrop bead. They work well with size 11/0 seed beads, but they are hard to find and come in a limited range of colors.

Variation

Blue Scalloped Peyote With Fringe Bracelet

This bracelet is worked in the same manner as the project, but it uses size 11/0 seed beads in place of the size 8/0 seed beads. Each side of the bracelet is a different color, which requires more color changes. The drop beads on the edge are the 8/0 Czech raindrop beads mentioned above. The smaller beads make a more elegant presentation.

Note:

Work this weave very loosely. To get the maximum benefit from the scallop, you want to be able to see a bit of space between the beads.

MATERIALS FOR A 7" (18cm) BRACELET

8lb FireLine or .008" diameter WildFire beading thread

Size 8/0 matte brown seed beads—about 250

Size 8/0 matte yellow seed beads—about 200

4mm drop bead designer mix in ambers and yellows—about 350

1" shank button—1

TOOLS

Size 10 beading needle—1

Scissors

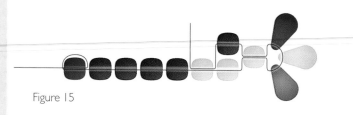

Figure 15

Making the Band

1 Single thread your needle with as much thread as you can handle.

2 Tie a waste bead within 8" (20cm) of the end of the thread.

3 Refer to the instructions for making the basic peyote band in the *Embellished Peyote Bracelet*, page 50.

4 Begin by threading on four brown and two yellow beads, as shown in Figure 15.

5 Pick up one yellow bead and three of the drop beads. Since the drop beads are a designer mix, pick up individual beads randomly for best results.

6 Pass the needle back through the yellow bead you picked up in step 5, as shown in Figure 15.

7 Pick up a brown bead and pass through the first yellow bead you picked up in step 4. Refer to Figure 15.

8 Pick up one yellow bead and pass through the third (brown) bead you picked up in step 4, as shown in Figure 16.

9 Continue to the end of the row, adding a brown bead, as shown in Figure 16.

10 Pick up one yellow bead and three drop beads (Figure 17). Pass back through the yellow bead.

11 Pick up one brown bead and start the next row, as shown in Figure 17.

Figure 16

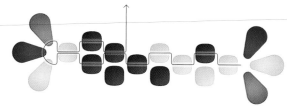

Figure 17

Figure 18

12 Continue across the row, picking up a yellow bead next and finishing with a brown bead, as shown in Figure 18.

13 Add a yellow bead and three drop beads and pass back through the yellow bead, as shown in Figure 18.

14 Keep in mind as you weave that you are making a diagonal line of yellow beads down the pattern. See Figure 19 (below) for the progression of the weave. Note that there are two yellow beads side by side on either side of the band where the diagonals meet. You can easily tell if you have placed a bead incorrectly, as the yellow beads will not be in a diagonal line.

15 Continue weaving back and forth, catching the drop beads on the side until you have the length you need. Be sure to weave an extra ½" to 1" (1cm to 3cm) beyond what you need, as the length will shorten as you make the scallop. Finish the yellow line of beads to the edge.

16 Leave the needle and thread to dangle in case you want to add or remove some beads after you make the scallop.

Making the Scallop

1 Cut 4' (1.2m) of thread and double thread your needle. Tie a waste bead 8" (20cm) from the end.

2 From one end of the band, pass the needle down the row of yellow beads diagonally to the other side of the band. Refer to Figure 19.

3 Repeat step 2 back and forth across the band, pulling the thread snug after each pass, as shown in Figure 19. Your band should start scalloping.

4 Work to the other end of the band and tie the thread off.

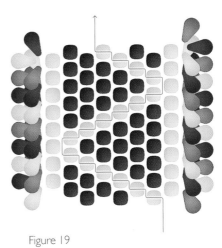

Figure 19

Finishing the Bracelet

1 Sew the button to one end of the band about ½" (1cm) from the end in the center of the band.

2 Make a loop at the other end of the band; the loop needs to be big enough to pass over the button.

3 Tie off all threads and secure them into the beading.

Chapter 4:

Square Stitch

I was really thrilled when I learned to do square stitch. In a former life I was a needlework designer and designed tons of cross-stitch and needlepoint. Square stitch looks a lot like both of those techniques, so it was a natural for me. It also looks exactly like loom beading.

The greatest benefit of square stitching over loom beading is that you don't have all those warp threads to work into your piece. The biggest downside to square stitch is that you work it one bead at a time, so it can be a slow process depending on the size of the beads you use. You can also increase and decrease square stitch, though I won't cover that here. (If you are interested in learning more about square stitch, check out *Beyond Beading Basics,* Krause Publications, 2009, for more information.)

The bracelets in this chapter use square stitch as a base to embellish upon. In the first bracelet, the square stitch can't even be seen.

I think you will find this stitch easy to learn and to use.

Caterpillar Bracelet with Peanut Beads

This bracelet is my version of a caterpillar bracelet—a bracelet usually made with a base of square or peyote stitched beads embellished on top with various-sized loops of seed and larger beads. This particular variation uses 4mm cube beads, size 11/0 seed beads, 2mm x 4mm peanut beads and a beautiful button clasp to make a lush presentation. Peanut beads are relatively new in the seed bead market; you might have to hunt a bit to find them, but they are well worth the effort.

This view of the back of the bracelet shows the square stitch base.

Variation

Wooly Bear Bracelet

Where I come from, Wooly Bears are black-and-tan caterpillars that are common in the late summer and fall. Old-timers claim to predict the severity of Midwestern winters based on the color and density of the Wooly Bear's coat. If this bracelet is any indication, it is going to be a hard winter.

In this version of the bracelet, drop beads were used in place of the peanut beads.

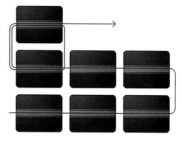

Figure 1

Making the Square Stitched Band

1 Cut as much thread as you can handle, and single thread your needle. You will have to add thread as you work. Plan to work in the tails as you proceed.

2 Tie a waste bead on the end of your thread, leaving a 6" (15cm) tail.

3 You will be making a band three cubes wide. Refer to the instructions for the square stitch strand in *Chapter 1: The Sampler Bracelet*, page 19.

4 Each time you complete a new row, pass the needle through the previous row and back through the one you just finished, as shown in Figure 1. This will reinforce the work and keep it even.

5 Add a seventh bead and continue weaving, as shown in Figure 2, until the band is the length you want. The ends of the band should just meet around your wrist.

6 When you are ready to do the last row, refer to Figure 3. Add one bead on the outside edge. The middle bead will be the shank of the button. Treat it like a bead. Then add the last bead in the row.

7 Pass back through the row below and the row with the button, as shown in Figure 4. Repeat this step several times to reinforce the button.

Figure 2

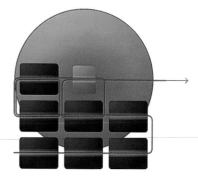

Figure 3

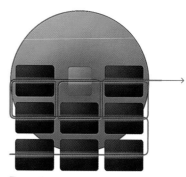

Figure 4

Making the Loops

1 When you come out of the second to last row on your last rein-forcing pass, take the needle through the outside bead of the last row, as shown in Figure 5.

2 Pick up two seed beads, one peanut bead, two seeds, one peanut, two seeds, one peanut and two seeds.

3 Make a loop around the first bead and pass through it again, as shown in Figure 5.

4 Pass through the button shank and third bead in the row. The button should flip over so it is on the right side of the bracelet.

5 Repeat step 2, passing around and back through the third bead, making a second loop, as shown in Figure 6.

6 Start the next row by passing the needle through the outside bead and picking up the beads as listed in step 2. Pass around and through the bead, as shown in Figure 6.

7 Continue across each row and down the length of the band. The peanut beads are a mix of colors, so use them randomly for the best effect.

8 Remove the waste bead and work the thread tail into the piece. Tie a few half hitch knots as you proceed, and trim any excess thread.

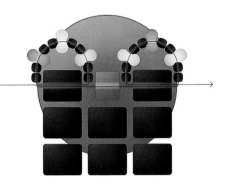

Figure 5

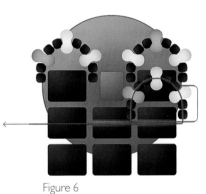

Figure 6

Finishing the Bracelet

1 When you are done adding all the loops, work your thread back around until it comes out through the middle bead of the third row from the end. Refer to Figure 7.

2 Pick up enough seed beads to make a loop long enough to capture the button. Make sure it passes over the button easily but not too loosely.

3 Keep in mind as you pass through the loop several more times to reinforce it that doing so will tighten it. Work the thread tail into the piece and trim any excess thread.

Figure 7

Mini Cubes Bracelet

Cube beads come in a variety of sizes from 1.5mm and up. These mini cubes appeal to me because of my experience as a needlework designer, and they remind me of the little squares on cross-stitch fabric. They do make a nice canvas for embellishment when woven into a band. This bracelet is a time guzzler, so don't expect to make it tonight and wear it tomorrow—it's just not going to happen!

I've provided a couple of ways to embellish it; experiment and see what you can come up with.

This view of the back of the bracelet shows how the mini cubes form a traditional square stitch base. Notice also the delicate seed bead picot.

Variation

Mini Cubes Bracelet With Lavender Crystals

The band in the lighter-colored version is ninety-three rows long. The embellishment on this bracelet starts by coming out one side at the loop end of the band and picking up six size 14/0 seed beads, one 4mm crystal, one size 14/0 seed bead, one crystal and six size 14/0 seed beads. Pass back into the band (on the same side) nine rows over. Pass the needle to the other side of the band and repeat. When you get to the other end, pass back along the bracelet, picking up six size 14/0 seed beads, pass through the crystal-seed-crystal pattern and pick up an additional six size 14/0 seed beads. Pass back through the band to the other side. Continue down the band.

MATERIALS FOR A 7" (18cm) BRACELET

6lb FireLine fishing line

1.8mm cube beads—6 to 7 grams

½" (1cm) shank button—1

Size 14/0 seed beads—4 grams

4mm bicone crystals—22

TOOLS

Size 10 or 12 beading needle—1

Scissors

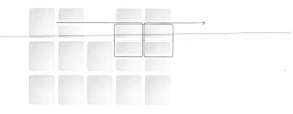

Figure 8

Making the Basic Band

1 Single thread your needle with as much thread as you can handle.

2 Tie a waste bead on the end of your thread, leaving an 8" (20cm) tail.

3 Refer to the instructions for making a square stitch band. See the *Caterpillar Bracelet, Making the Square Stitched Band*, page 60. Instead of using three of the larger cubes as directed in those instructions, use five of the mini cubes, and take them to the end of your thread.

4 Remember to pass back through the previous row and the one you just finished as you complete each row, in order to reinforce and align the beads.

5 Continue weaving as above until you are three rows short of meeting around your wrist.

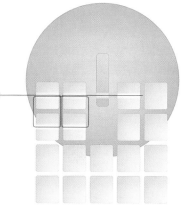

Figure 9

Adding the Button

1 Weave in the first two beads of the next row, as shown in Figure 8. Skip the third bead and weave in the remaining two beads, as shown. Your thread will show between beads. Be sure to pass back through the rows to reinforce.

2 Weave the first two beads of the next row in place. Pass through the shank of the button. Finish the row as usual. Refer to Figure 9.

3 For the final row, refer to Figure 10, and repeat what you did in step 2. Pass through the last two rows several times to reinforce the button. Tie off the thread securely.

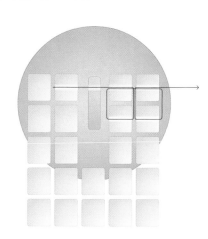

Figure 10

Adding the Surface Embellishment

1 Secure a new thread in the end of the band without the button.

2 Refer to Figure 11, and bring the thread out one side of the very last row.

3 Pick up five seed beads, one crystal and five seed beads, as shown in Figure 11.

4 Count over five rows diagonally and pass through the band, as shown in Figure 11.

5 Repeat step 3.

6 Continue across the band close to the button end. You may not come out clear to the end of the band but that's alright, since the button hides the end of the bracelet.

7 When you get to the end of your patterns, pass across the band. Pick up five seed beads, pass into the crystal, as shown in Figure 12, and pick up five more seed beads. Pass through the band and repeat. Refer to Figure 12. You should be making X's across the band.

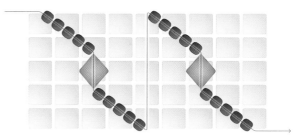

Figure 11

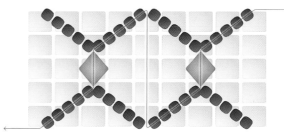

Figure 12

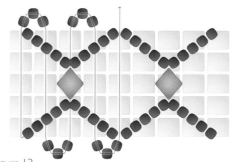

Figure 13

Adding the Picot Edge

1 Again, start at the end of the band, as shown in Figure 13.

2 Pick up three seed beads, and pass the needle through the next row, as shown in Figure 13.

3 Pick up three seeds and pass the needle through the next row. Continue this for the length of the band, as shown in Figure 13.

Adding the Loop

1 Bring your thread out of the band three rows from the end without the button.

2 Make a loop big enough to pass over the button. Refer to Figure 14.

3 Pass through the loop several times to reinforce. Tie off the threads.

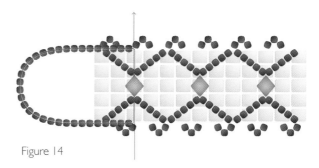

Figure 14

Chapter 5

Triangle Weave

Triangle weave is a three-sided bead pattern. It is done in the same manner as single needle, right-angle weave but with three beads instead of four. Each new pattern is comprised of two beads and one bead of the previous pattern. The result is a pattern that resembles rickrack. The patterns can be woven into a circle and made into beaded beads. The weave by itself makes a nice beaded chain but can also be combined with other stitches or woven into itself to make stunning bracelets, as the projects in this chapter prove.

If you find this stitch to be confusing, do not feel alone. There is something about three-sided patterns that are difficult to see at first. Part of it is that the pattern moves in a zigzag instead of a straight line. Keep playing with it and it will come to you.

Triangles & Crosses Bracelet

My bead stash is loaded at the moment with lots of 4mm bicone crystals and fire polish beads. While playing around with them, I came up with this bracelet. It's done in a simple triangle weave that results in a zigzag pattern. Two bands of zigzag are then joined together with seed beads to form a wide cuff. A simple button and loop closure finish off the project. Make the bracelet in one color of beads, or try making it with bands of different colors. Play around with your color choices and see what happens.

Variation

Triangles & Crosses Bracelet in Two Colors

The pattern for this bracelet is the same as the pattern in the project. This bracelet, however, uses two colors of crystals instead of one. This bracelet can be made with fire polish or other beads.

MATERIALS FOR A 7" (18cm) BRACELET

.008" (02mm) diameter Beadalon DandyLine beading thread—4 yards

4mm bicone crystals—194 or fire polish beads—162

Size 14/0 seed beads—2 grams

¾" (2cm) shank button—1

TOOLS

Size 10 or 12 beading needles—2

Scissors

Glue

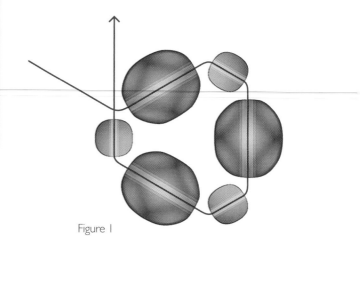

Figure 1

Making the Bands

1 Cut 2 yards (1.8m) of thread and single thread your needle.

2 Pick up one crystal, one seed, one crystal, one seed, one crystal and one seed and take them to within 8" (20cm) of the end of the thread. Refer to Figure 1.

3 Pass the needle back through the first three beads you picked up (crystal, seed and crystal). Refer to Figure 2. Pull the thread snug through the beads.

4 Pick up one crystal, one seed, one crystal and one seed.

5 Pass back through the crystal you exited from in step 3 and the first new crystal you picked up in step 4. Refer to Figure 3. Pull the thread snug.

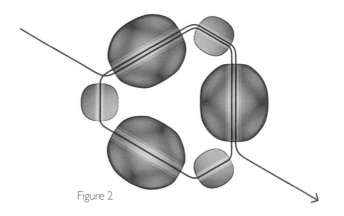

Figure 2

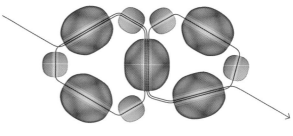

Figure 3

6 Next pick up one crystal, one seed, one crystal and one seed.

7 Pass back through the crystal you exited in step 5 and the first crystal you picked up in step 6. Refer to Figure 4. Pull the thread snug.

8 Your first three patterns should look like Figure 5.

9 Repeat steps 6 and 7 until you have a length that goes around your wrist and just meets. See the progression of the weave in Figure 6. Be sure you have the same number of points (the seed-crystal-seed pattern that forms) on each edge of the band. Leave all thread tails intact and set aside.

10 Repeat steps 1 through 9 for the second band.

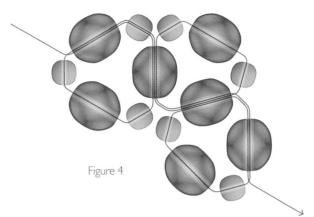

Figure 4

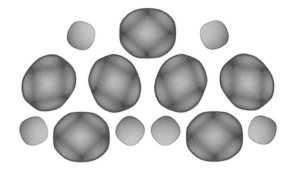

Figure 5

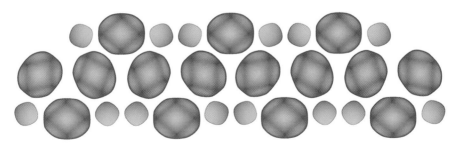

Figure 6

Weaving the Bands Together: First Pass

1 Lay the bands on a flat surface. Each band should have a thread tail on one end and the working thread and needle on the other. Lay the bands lengthwise side by side with the working thread of each pointing in the opposite direction. Be sure the points line up.

2 On one band, work the thread around through the seed and first crystal point bead (skipping the second seed). Refer to Figure 7.

3 Pick up five seed beads and pass through the second point bead (no seeds) on the second band. Refer to Figure 7.

4 Pick up five seed beads and pass through the third point bead on the first band. Refer to Figure 7.

5 Pick up five more seed beads and pass through the fourth point bead on the second band.

6 Continue in this manner to the other end of the band.

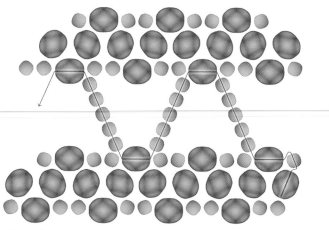

Figure 7

Weaving the Bands Together: Second Pass

1 On band two, pass the working thread around until it comes out of the first point bead on that end. Refer to Figure 8.

2 Pick up two seed beads. Pass through the middle bead of the five seeds from the first pass. Refer to Figure 8.

3 Pick up two more seed beads and pass into the second point bead on the first band. Refer to Figure 8.

4 Pick up two seed beads. Pass through the middle bead of the five from the second pass. Refer to Figure 8.

5 Pick up two more seed beads and pass into the third point bead on the second band. Refer to Figure 8.

6 Continue in this manner to the end of the band.

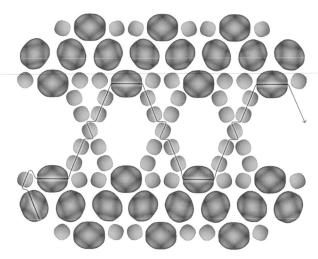

Figure 8

Adding the Button

1 You should have two threads on each end of each band. Work them around until they come out at the same place on the end of the band. Refer to Figure 9.

2 Place both threads in the needle. Trim the threads so they are the same length.

3 On the first end, pick up two or three seed beads, the button and another two or three seed beads. Refer to Figure 9.

4 Pass across the band and into the crystal on the opposite side. Refer to Figure 9.

5 Work around the pattern, making half hitch knots as you go. Do this for several patterns.

6 Place glue on the thread and pass it through another bead. Trim the thread ends.

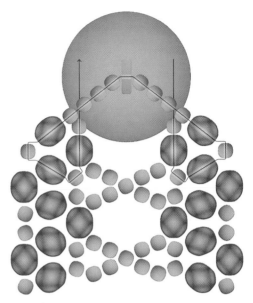

Figure 9

Adding the Loop

1 On other end, work the threads around until they come out the same place on the end of the band. Refer to Figure 10.

2 Pick up enough seed beads to pass around the button comfortably but without being loose.

3 Pass across the band and into the crystal on the opposite side. Refer to Figure 10.

4 Work around the pattern, making half hitch knots as you go. Do this for several patterns.

5 Place glue on the thread and pass it through another bead. Trim the thread ends.

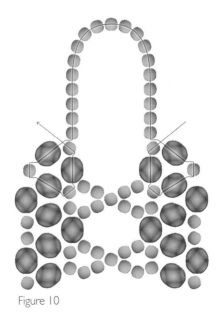

Figure 10

Triangles & Diamonds Bracelet

One afternoon I was experimenting with seed beads, trying to come up with a new bracelet idea using the triangle stitch. I wondered if I could figure out a way to weave it into itself and make a diamond-shaped pattern. The result of my endeavors is the purple bracelet variation of this project. The bracelet consists of two bands that are joined using a right-angle weave stitch and matte seed beads down the center. Even though I was very pleased with my endeavors, time constraints led me onto something else and the bracelet went into a drawer with other possible projects, and I forgot all about it until I started writing this book.

For the purposes of this book I decided to just make one band and to use larger beads. Alternating the colors of the beads makes the diamond pattern stand out so it is more obvious. Making the bracelet in one color makes a very attractive project too.

Variations

Triangles & Diamonds Pink Bracelet

This pink bracelet is the same as the black and white one with the addition of size 14/0 seed beads between the fire polish beads.

Triangles & Diamonds Blue Bracelet

The blue bracelet is the same as the project but woven in only one color. The diamond pattern is less obvious.

Triangles & Diamonds Purple Seed Beads Bracelet

This is the original bracelet I came up with while experimenting. This bracelet consists of two bands woven in the same manner as in the project but featuring seed beads in place of the fire polish beads. The two bands are joined together with a right-angle weave stitch.

MATERIALS FOR AN 8" (20cm) BRACELET

6lb white FireLine fishing line or .008" (.2mm) diameter white WildFire beading thread

4mm white fire polish beads—66

4mm black fire polish beads—80

4mm red bicone crystals—19

Size 11/0 black seed beads—1 gram

⅝" (16mm) black shank button—1

TOOLS

Size 10 or 12 beading needles—2

Scissors

Making the First Band

1 Cut 1½ (1.4m) yards of thread and single thread your needle.

2 Refer to steps 1 through 10 on pages 70–71, *Triangles & Crosses Bracelet, Making the Bands*. Omit the seed beads from those directions and instead start with a white bead and alternate groupings of white and black fire polish beads. Weave a band long enough to go around your wrist. Refer to Figure 11.

3 End the band with a white pattern (Figure 11). Leave the threads hanging at both ends of the band.

Joining the Second Band to the First

1 Cut 1½ yards (1.4m) of thread and single thread your needle.

2 Pick up three white beads and pass through the first two beads again, making a triangle pattern (Figure 12, black line).

3 Pick up a black bead and pass through the lower black bead of the first band (Figure 12, green line). Pass back through the white bead you exited and the black one you just picked up (Figure 12, green line). Pull up snug.

4 Pick up two black beads and pass back through the black bead you picked up in step 3 (Figure 12, red line). Pass back through the first black bead you picked up in this step (Figure 12, red line).

5 Pick up one white bead and pass through the black bead from the first band and the first black bead you picked up in the last pass (Figure 12, purple line). Pass through the white bead again.

6 Pick up two white beads and pass back through the white bead you picked up in the last pass (Figure 12, blue line). Pass back through the first white bead you picked up (Figure 12, blue line).

7 Continue weaving down the band to the end, picking up the colors of beads you need to make the pattern. It is very easy to determine if you make a mistake as you weave.

8 Leave the thread tails hanging.

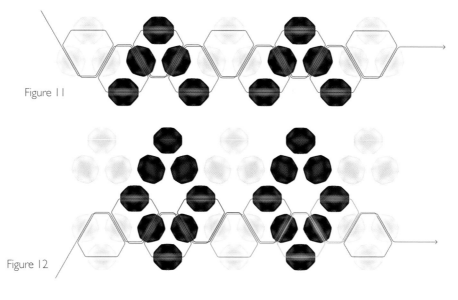

Figure 11

Figure 12

Adding the Crystal Beads

1 Cut 2' (.6m) of thread and single thread your needle. Tie a waste bead about 8" (20cm) from the end.

2 Pass through the first black bead in the center of the band and pick up a crystal (Figure 13).

3 Repeat step 2 across the center of the band.

4 Work the ending thread through the beading and tie it off.

5 Remove the waste bead and work the thread through the beading and tie it off.

Finishing the Bracelet

1 There should be a thread coming out of each end of each band (4 threads). Place a needle on each ending thread on one end of the bracelet.

2 On one needle, pick up three black seed beads, the button and three black seed beads (Figure 14, red line). Pass into the beading on the other side of the band.

3 Work the thread around the pattern and back through the beads to the other side.

4 Pass the second needle through the three seed beads, the button and the three seed beads to the opposite side (Figure 14, green line).

5 Work the thread around the pattern and back through the beads to the other side.

6 Weave both thread tails through the work, tying half hitch knots as you weave. Trim the thread ends.

7 Place a needle in each ending thread on the other end of the bracelet.

8 On one needle pick up enough seed beads to make a loop big enough to pass easily over the button (Figure 15, red line). Pass into the beads on the other side of the band. Work around the pattern and back through the beads to the first side.

9 Pass the second needle through the loop of beads from the other side (Figure 15, green line). Pass into the beads on the other side of the band. Work around the pattern and back through the beads to the first side.

10 Weave both thread tails through the work, tying half hitch knots as you weave. Trim the thread ends.

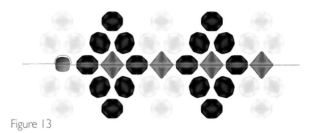

Figure 13

Figure 14

Figure 15

Chapter 6:

Brick Stitch

In all the years I've been beading, I had never tried brick stitch (also called Comanche stitch, as it has Native American origins). But no book on bead-woven bracelets would be complete without including this stitch, so I had to teach myself how to do it. I am admitting in print that I am far from an expert on this particular stitch.

Brick looks a lot like peyote stitch when completed, and you can achieve very similar results with it. In fact, it is often hard to tell which of the two stitches a woven piece was done in. The major difference between the two stitches is that in brick stitch each new bead is woven into the thread that bridges the beads from the *adjoining row* instead of from the beads from *that* row.

Brick stitch is usually started using a ladder of bugle, hex or seed beads, as in the **Black & Purple Trapezoids Bracelet**. The two center rows of that bracelet are done in ladder stitch. Brick stitch is done on either side of the two center rows. There are ways of starting brick stitch without the ladder but they won't be covered here. There are also a number of interesting chains you can make using brick stitch; the first project in this chapter uses one of them.

Alternating Brick Stitch Bracelet

I want to thank Beth Stone, author of **Seed Bead Stitching** (Kalmbach Books, 2007), for the inspiration for this bracelet. I found the instructions for the stitch in her book, and I tried it and really liked doing it. The stitch by itself is not very wide when done in size 11/0 and size 8/0 seed beads, but two strands woven together with a lacing of 4mm crystals makes for a very nice ⅝" (16mm) wide band. It is easy to join the bands with seed beads and to add a button and loop closure. You can also add a purchased clasp if you prefer.

My beading mantra—the way I choose colors and beads—involves a lot of contrast: matte against shiny, texture against smooth and light against dark. I may use some or all of those in a project. For this project I chose matte against shiny. There is a hint of brown in the matte AB 8/0 seed beads, which is emphasized by the amber crystals. Choose the colors you prefer and give this bracelet a try.

Variations

Blue Alternating Brick Stitch Bracelet

This bracelet uses 4mm bicone crystals, with four 11/0 seed beads for each bicone on the outer bands. The bands are joined together with crosses made of hot pink size 14/0 seed beads; every crystal in the inside of each band is woven through in this manner.

Pink Alternating Brick Stitch Bracelet

Changing the size of the beads drastically alters the look of the weave in this bracelet. Milky pink crystals are joined with pastel metallic size 11/0 and size 8/0 seed beads in this wide cuff. The bands are again joined together with crosses.

MATERIALS FOR A 7" (18cm) BRACELET

6lb FireLine fishing line or .006" (.15mm) diameter WildFire beading thread

Size 8/0 matte green AB seed beads—4 grams

Size 11/0 matte green seed beads—4 grams

Size 14/0 black seed beads—1 gram

4mm amber bicone crystals—30

½" (1cm) bronze shank button—1

TOOLS

Size 10 or 12 beading needles—2

Scissors

Making the Bands

1 Single thread your needle with 1½ yards (1.4m) of thread.

2 Follow the instructions in *Chapter 1: The Sampler Bracelet, The Alternating Brick Stitch Strand*, steps 1 through 6 on page 21, to weave a band using the size 11/0 and size 8/0 seed beads.

3 Make the band three patterns longer than it takes to meet around your wrist. Leave the threads dangling; you will weave them in later.

4 Repeat steps 1 through 3 for the second band. Make sure it is the same length.

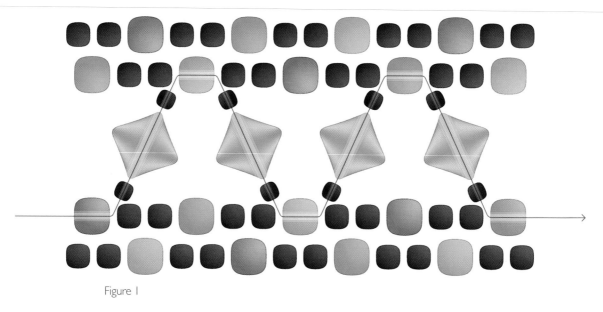

Figure 1

Weaving the Bands Together

1 Thread your needle with a yard of thread and tie a waste bead 8" (20cm) from the end.

2 Beginning at the left end of the lower band (or right if you prefer), pass through the first size 8/0 seed bead (Figure 1).

3 Pick up one size 14/0 seed bead, one bicone crystal, and one size 14/0 seed bead. Pass diagonally across the band and pass through the second size 8/0 seed from the end on the upper band (Figure 1).

4 Pick up one size 14/0 seed, one bicone crystal, and one size 14/0 seed. Pass diagonally across the band and pass through the third size 8/0 seed from the end on the lower band (Figure 1).

5 Continue repeating steps 3 and 4 across the band using every other size 8/0 seed bead until you are three patterns from the end.

6 Check for fit. Work the thread out through band, remove the needle and let the thread hang.

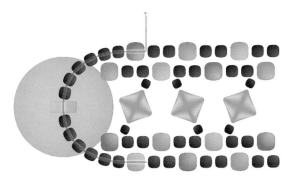

Figure 2

Adding the Button

1 You should have threads hanging off each band at the end where you started. Put the threads from each side on separate needles.

2 On the "red" needle (see Figure 2), pick up three seed beads, the button and three seed beads. You may need more or fewer seed beads depending on the shank of your button.

3 Pass across the band into the size 11/0 beads on the other side. Work through the beads, following the pattern and tying half hitch knots as you proceed. Trim the thread tails.

4 With the "black" needle (see Figure 2), pass though the loop of beads and button shank to the other side.

5 Repeat step 3.

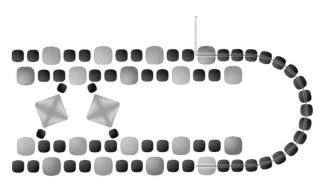

Figure 3

Adding the Loop

1 On other end of the bracelet, put the threads from each side on separate needles.

2 On the "red" needle (see Figure 3), pick up enough seed beads to make a loop big enough to pass over your button. Remember, you should have three extra patterns to use as part of the loop. Check for fit before proceeding.

3 Pass the thread into the weaving on the other side of the band and tie off with half hitch knots. Trim the thread ends.

4 Pass the "black" needle (see Figure 3) through the loop of beads you added and into the weaving on the other band.

5 Repeat step 3.

Black & Purple Trapezoids Bracelet

There are a number of ways to start brick stitch. The traditional way is with a ladder stitch. The bracelet in this project is started with a double row of ladder stitch down the middle, with a band of brick stitch off each side. The beads in brick stitch are usually referred to as "stacks" because you can use one or more beads at a time in a stack. The beads in this bracelet are size 8/0 hex and are fairly large, so I only used one bead per stack.

The center two rows of ladder stitch form the basis of the pattern—the tops and bottoms of the trapezoids. You may weave your ladder in either the one or two needle method—both will work. Just keep in mind that you will be adding two beads at a time in each stack of your ladder.

The finishing touch on this bracelet is the single bead finish over the edge to hide the thread. This is done with a simple whip stitch through the threads between the beads.

Variation

Blue & Purple Brick Bracelet

This blue and purple bracelet is done in brick stitch in a similar pattern to the project. Instead of size 8/0 hex beads, this variation was made with size 10/0 Delica beads. As you can see, brick and peyote stitches resemble each other a bit.

MATERIALS FOR A 7" (18cm) BRACELET

6lb FireLine fishing line or .006" (.15mm) diameter WildFire beading thread

Size 8/0 hex rose/gold luster beads—10 grams

Size 8/0 hex black opaque beads—10 grams

Copper clamshell bead tips—2

Crimp beads—2

Copper snap clasp—1

TOOLS

Size 10 or 12 beading needles—2

Scissors

Round-nose pliers

Making the Ladder

1 Follow the instructions given in *Chapter 1: The Sampler Bracelet, The Ladder Stitch Strand*, page 24, and make a ladder using both colors of hex beads in a two-bead stack (Figure 4). You may use whichever method (one needle or two needle) you prefer.

2 You will do five stacks with the black bead on top and the rose luster bead on the bottom.

3 Switch and do three stacks with the rose luster bead on top and the black bead on the bottom.

4 Repeat steps 2 and 3 seven more times. If you need to add or remove patterns for length, do so in this step.

5 Repeat step 2. You want to end the bracelet so it makes a point on the end, so it needs to end the way you started. Refer to the photo on page 85.

Starting the Brick Stitch

1 To begin the first row of brick stitch, you need to have the thread coming out of the top of the base row. If your thread is coming out of the bottom, simply flip the band over. If you used two threads to make the ladder, leave the bottom one hanging (to use when you do the other side). You need the thread to come out of a black bead.

2 The illustrations show the progress of the work from left to right. Bring your thread up from the base and pick up two black beads (Figure 5).

Figure 4

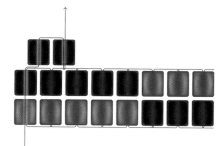

Figure 5

3 Skip the first thread between the first two beads of the ladder row and pass your needle under the second thread and back up through the second bead (Figure 5).

4 Pass the thread back through the first bead and back up through the second (Figure 6).

5 From this point on you will add one bead at a time by picking up the bead, passing through the thread loop between the beads in the ladder row and back up through the bead you just added (Figure 7).

6 As you progress in this row, you will add one less black bead and add one extra purple bead (see Figure 8) so you are alternately adding four of each bead across this row.

7 You will end the row one half of a bead short. Flip the band over and start the next row as you did in steps 2 through 4.

8 Follow the pattern (Figure 8) for bead placement. Note that the pattern has reversed itself so now there are five purple and three black beads in this row.

9 Repeat steps 2 through 8 for the other side of the bracelet.

Adding the Edging

1 Bring the thread out of the end bead (Figure 9), and pick up a bead; be sure to alternate the colors of the beads on the edging with those on the band (see the photo on page 85).

2 Pass the needle through the loop of thread between the first two beads (Figure 9).

3 Pick up another bead and pass the needle through the loop of thread between the next two beads (Figure 9).

4 Continue across the band to the other end. Work the thread tails into the piece and tie them off. Trim the thread ends.

5 Repeat steps 1 through 4 for the other side.

Adding the Clasp

1 Place a needle on each end of 18" (46cm) of thread. Starting several patterns back from the end of the ladder stitch row, work the thread through the beads following the pattern to the end of the bracelet.

2 Bring the two threads out between the beads in the middle two rows at one end of the bracelet (Figure 9).

3 Pass both threads through a clamshell bead tip from the bottom and up (see page 13 for instructions).

4 Thread a crimp bead on one needle and tie off the threads against the crimp. Close the clamshell.

5 Repeat steps 1 through 4 for the other end.

6 Attach the clamshell to the clasp with round-nose pliers.

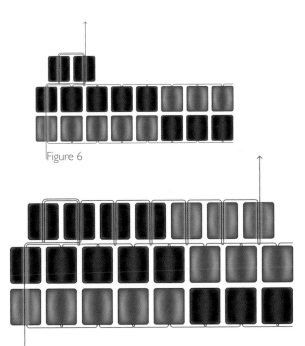

Figure 6

Figure 7

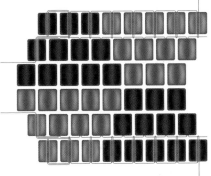

Figure 8

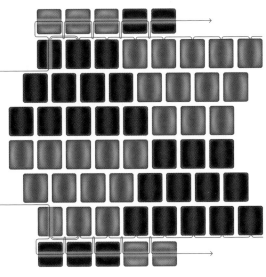

Figure 9

Chapter 7:

Netting Stitch

Most off-loom beading could technically be called netting, but for our purposes here we are referring to netting as the regular or irregular open-bead fabric that results when one or more beads are joined to a previous row, resulting in a pattern of openings. The regular weave results in a pattern of alternating diamonds. It is an easy stitch to learn and to use.

The weave is done with one thread and can be done horizontally, vertically or randomly. The beads in the weave are called bridge and shared beads. The shared beads are ones that join patterns and have two threads running through them. The bridge beads are the ones between and only have one thread running through them. The pattern is usually done with a number of bridge beads in one color followed by a shared bead in a contrasting or different color.

Netting makes a great base for projects like bracelets and can be easily embellished. It works well to encase objects that you would like to hold in place like cabochons. Netting is also an excellent stitch to use to cover three-dimensional objects like Christmas ornaments.

For more in-depth information on netting, check out Diane Fitzgerald's **Netted Beadwork** (Interweave Press, 2003).

Flower Clasp Bracelet

This bracelet utilizes both horizontal and vertical netting: the band is done in horizontal and the flower in vertical. But it is the clasp on this bracelet that is the star of the piece and should be worn as the focal point, on top of the wrist.

This bracelet looks a lot harder than it actually is. You only have one needle to deal with, and netting is an up and down or back and forth pattern depending on which direction you work. You will, however, need to do a lot of counting as both the band and the flower are done in five-bead netting. Start with the band. Seeing the pattern that results when you pass through the contrasting shared bead will help you understand the weave before doing it all in one color on the flower.

So choose your favorite colors and get to work.

Variation

Flower Clasp Bracelet in Denim

This bracelet is the same pattern as the pink and green bracelet, but it uses a designer seed bead mix in denim colors. It is done in the three-bead pattern. There are no contrasting shared beads, so that makes the pattern more difficult to do and to differentiate. The flower is done much the same except that an orange crystal bicone was attached in the middle for a hint of a contrasting color.

MATERIALS FOR A 7" (18cm) BRACELET

6lb FireLine fishing line or .006" (.15mm) diameter WildFire beading thread

Size 11/0 clear pink-lined seed beads—5 grams

Size 11/0 olive silver-lined seed beads—8 grams

TOOLS

Size 10 or 12 beading needle—1

Scissors

Making the Band

1 Cut as much thread as you can handle and single thread your needle.

2 Tie a pink bead within 10" (25cm) of the end of the thread. Refer to Figure 1.

3 Begin threading on two green beads followed by one pink until you have forty-one sets of two green beads. End with a pink bead. This is a five-bead pattern (two green, one pink and two green comprise one pattern).

4 If you need to change the length of the bracelet, do so by singles or multiples of the five-bead pattern. You will need to end with a half pattern to get it to turn correctly, which is why you had forty-one sets of green beads.

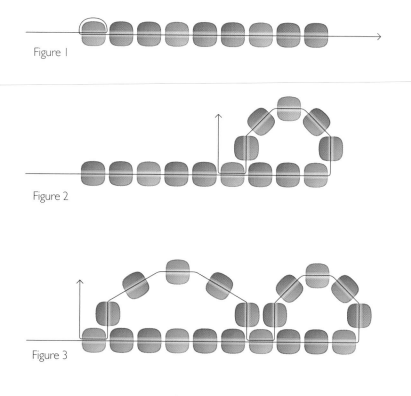

Figure 1

Figure 2

Figure 3

5 When you get the length you need and are ready to start the second row, pick up two green, one pink and two green beads, as shown in Figure 2.

6 Pass the thread through the second to last pink bead you picked up in the initial row of beads. Refer to Figure 2. Pull snug, making a loop.

7 Pick up two green, one pink and two green beads. Refer to Figure 3. Skip the next two-one-two bead pattern in the initial row and pass the thread through the next pink bead. Pull snug.

8 Continue repeating step 7 until you are within one pattern of the other end of the initial row.

9 Pick up the last five-bead pattern of the second row and pass the needle through the first pink bead you tied on in row 1. Refer to Figure 4. You may work the beginning thread tail in now and tie it off, or you can wait until later.

10 To turn the corner and start the third row, pick up two green, one pink and two green beads, and pass through the last pink bead you picked up in the second row. Refer to Figure 5.

11 Pick up two green, one pink and two green beads and pass through the upper pink bead in the next pattern in the row, as shown in Figure 6.

12 Continue working up and down the piece following the above instructions until you have completed nine rows of weaving. Tie off the threads and set the band aside.

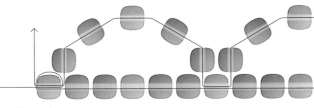

Figure 4

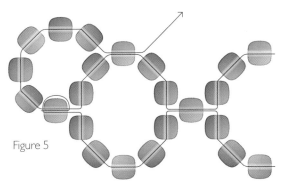

Figure 5

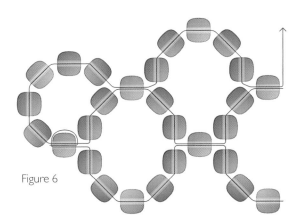

Figure 6

Making the Flower

1 Cut 1 yard (.9m) of thread and single thread your needle. Tie a pink bead within 6" (15cm) of the end of the thread. (The flower is worked in one color of pink beads but the diagrams are shown in two colors of pink to make it easier to differentiate the shared and bridge beads.)

Figure 7

2 Thread on an additional eleven pink beads for the first row. Refer to Figure 7.

3 Skip the last bead and pass back through the second to last bead, as shown in Figure 7. Pull snug so the bottom bead lies crosswise, making a picot (a decorative edge).

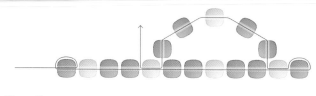

Figure 8

4 Pick up five beads and pass through the eighth bead from the bottom, as shown in Figure 8, and pull snug.

5 Thread on four more beads, as shown in Figure 9.

6 Skip the last bead and pass the thread through the second to last bead, as shown in Figure 9, making a picot, and pull snug.

Figure 9

7 Pick up five beads and pass through the eighth bead from the top, as shown in Figure 10, and pull snug.

8 Pick up four pink beads. Skip the last bead and pass back through the second from the bottom, as shown in Figure 11, making a picot.

9 Continue following steps 3 through 8, working up and down the piece, until you have thirty-six to forty point beads (the more point beads, the fuller your flower will be) at the top and bottom edges of the piece. The beginning and ending points will not be completed patterns. Tie off the beginning thread and bury the tail in the work. You will continue to use the remaining, working thread.

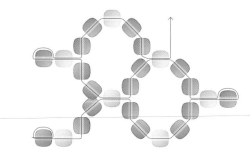

Figure 10

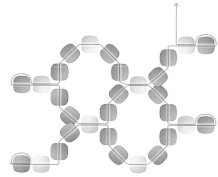

Figure 11

10 Pass the needle back through all the beads on the end of the band and through the point bead on the other side.

11 Run the thread through all the point beads on this edge and gather. Knot the thread between the beads to hold the gather in place.

12 Roll the first five beads around in a circle and secure.

13 Sew two point beads to each bead in the five-bead circle and repeat as you widen the circle.

Finishing the Bracelet

1 Sew the flower base to one end of the netted band.

2 On the other end, work a new thread into the woven band about an inch (3cm) back from the opposite end. See the photo below for placement.

3 Bring the thread out near the middle of the band and thread on enough beads to make a loop big enough to pass around the flower.

4 Work the thread back into the band, work around the pattern and pass through the loop again to reinforce.

The finished flower is hand sewn to the netted bracelet base.

Double Ruffles Bracelet

The ruffled stitch used in this bracelet is an old Native American stitch credited to the Lakota Nation. It is normally used alone so the stitch twists around itself. This bracelet starts out with four rows of the basic band you did in the *Flower Clasp Bracelet* (see page 80) and continues with consecutive rows of radical increases done on each side to make the ruffles. Handmade lampworked beads by Tanya McGuire form the bead clasp and add decorative accents around the base band.

Variation

Double Ruffles Bracelets in Pink & Yellow

The pink ruffled bracelet is done on a base band four rows wide like the project bracelet. Instead of adding decorative beads down the center like in the main project, another ruffle was added. The three shades of pink beads all have the same darker shade of bead for the shared bead. A toggle clasp finishes this bracelet.

The yellow bracelet has a center band two rows wide done in the darkest shade, which was also used for the first row of ruffle. The two successive rows are woven in lighter shades. The finishing touch on this bracelet is a row of 6mm bicone crystals attached down the center of the bracelet. A tiny snap clasp finishes this bracelet.

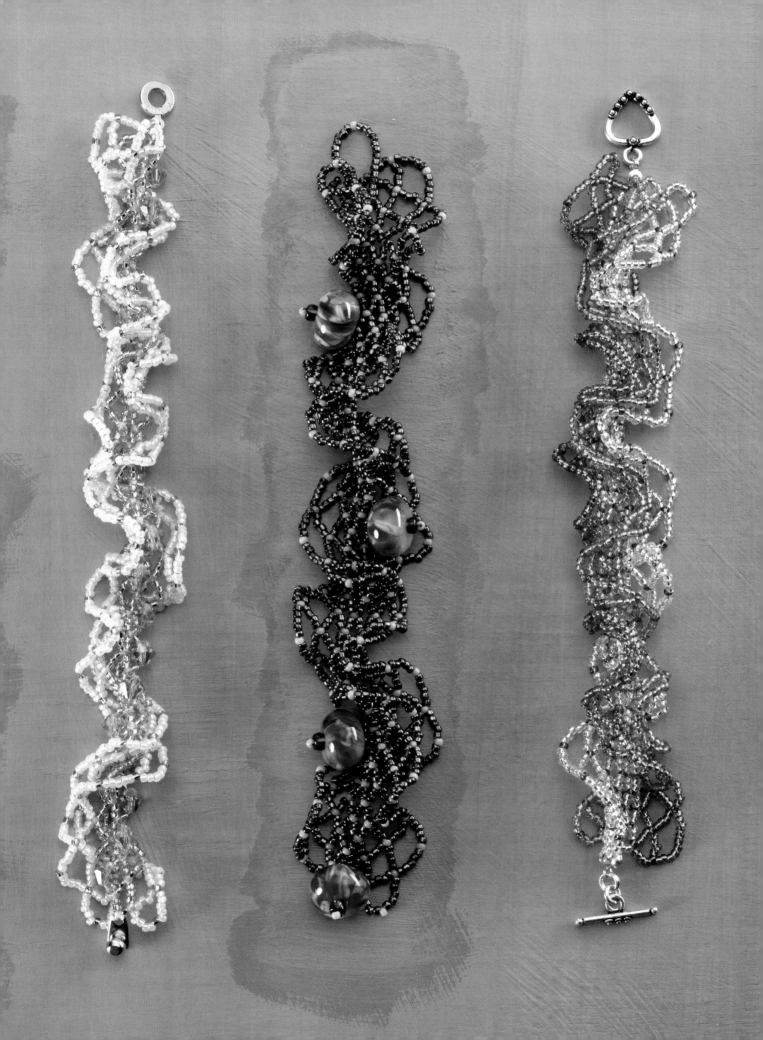

MATERIALS FOR A 7" (18cm) BRACELET

8lb FireLine fishing line

Size 11/0 medium blue AB seed beads—20 grams

Size 11/0 light blue opaque seed beads—5 grams

10mm × 15mm blue lampwork beads—4

Size 6/0 blue seed beads—4

TOOLS

Size 10 beading needle—1

Scissors

Figure 12

Figure 13

Making the Base Band

1 Follow instructions 1 through 12 under *Flower Clasp Bracelet, Making the Band*, pages 92-93. Use blue AB beads in place of the green beads and light blue beads in place of the pink beads. Make the band four rows wide. Do not cut off the thread.

Adding the Ruffles

1 Bring the thread out of the light blue shared bead at the end of the row and pick up three medium blue beads, one light blue and three medium blue. Skip the next light blue bead in the base band and pass the needle through the third light blue bead from the end. Refer to Figure 12.

2 Continue across the band in the same manner adding the three-one-three bead pattern until you come to the other end.

3 Always turn the row using the amount of beads you are going to use in the following row. Pick up four medium blue, one light blue and four medium blue beads and pass into the middle light blue bead in the first loop of the previous row. Refer to Figure 13.

4 Continue picking up four medium blue, one light blue and four medium blue beads as you pass along the row. Refer to Figure 14.

5 Turn the next corner using five medium blue, one light blue and five medium blue beads and pass into the first light blue bead, as shown in Figure 15.

6 Continue adding the five-one-five bead pattern across the row to the other end. Refer to Figure 16.

7 Tie off the thread and bury the tail in the work. Trim.

8 Repeat steps 1 through 7 for the other side of the band.

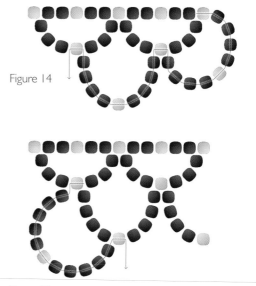

Figure 14

Figure 15

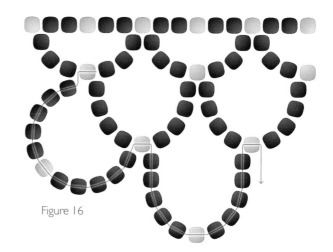

Figure 16

Adding the Bead Clasp

1 Tie a new thread into the work towards one end of the band. Bring the needle out between the two medium blue beads in the center half diamond on the edge, as shown in Figure 17.

2 Thread on two medium blue beads, enough beads to pass through the lampworked bead, one size 6/0 blue seed bead and one light blue seed, as shown in Figure 17.

3 Skip the last bead and pass back through the size 6/0 bead and the beads that pass through the lampworked bead.

4 Pick up two medium blue beads and pass through the light blue bead in the middle of the two diamond patterns, as shown in Figure 17.

5 Work the thread through the pattern and around to where you started and pass through all the beads again. Work the thread into the band and tie off using half hitch knots. Trim the tail.

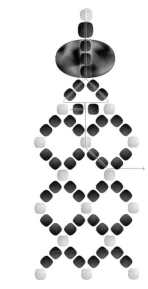

Figure 17

Adding the Decorative Beads

1 Divide and mark the band equally by the number of beads you have to sew on. Work your thread through the pattern to the first place you want to attach a bead. Refer to Figure 18.

2 Bring the needle up through the light blue bead at the point of one of the diamonds. Repeat the steps you used to attach the clasp bead. Pass around the diamond and back up through the beads to reinforce.

3 Work your thread through the pattern to your next marked place and repeat step 1. Continue until you have all your beads attached.

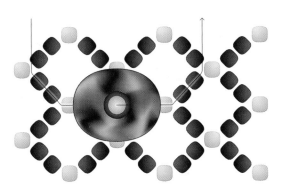

Figure 18

Making the Loop

1 Work your thread through the band to the other end coming out one diamond short of the end of the band, as shown in Figure 19.

2 Pick up enough beads to make a loop big enough to pass easily around your bead clasp, but not too loose.

3 Work around the pattern and come back out where you attached the loop and pass through the loop beads again to reinforce.

4 Work the thread tails through the piece, tying half hitch knots as you work. Bury the thread tails and trim.

Figure 19

Chapter 8:

Herringbone (Ndebele) Weave

The herringbone stitch is normally credited to the Ndebele people of South Africa. The weave produces columns of paired beads that incline towards each other at the bottom and away from each other at the top, forming a herringbone pattern. Because of the chevron or V shape of the beadwork, the herringbone is very conducive to making narrow tubes, as in the first project, *Herringbone Rope with Art Glass Bead* (page 102).

Although there are ways to do herringbone without a base, when done flat, the herringbone stitch is often worked on a base of ladder stitch like brick stitch. You will need to weave your ladder in an even number of beads since the herringbone is done in pairs of beads.

As with the other stitches we've covered so far, there are entire volumes written on Ndebele. I suggest you check them out if you want to explore this stitch further.

Many years ago, I took a class on herringbone stitch from Cheryl Erickson, owner of Artistic Bead and a nationally known beading instructor. Her class project was a rope bracelet that used triangle beads which fit very nicely together to make a smooth rope. Since I like a lot of texture in my projects, I decided to play around with other beads to see what I might come up with. This bracelet is one result of that experimentation.

Interspersing different sizes of beads throughout the weave produces an interesting undulating effect. The inclusion of the art glass bead (by Tanya McGuire) provides a focal point and adds a delicious inspiration for the colors chosen for this bracelet.

Variation

Green Herringbone Rope Bracelet

This bracelet is done the same way as the project but without the large art bead. The size 11/0 bead sections are the same length but are alternated with the bead band comprised of sizes 8/0, 6/0 and 8/0 beads and a single size 8/0 bead band.

Note:

Because this bracelet is a rope, it needs to be longer to go around your wrist. Allow at least 1¾" (4cm) more than your wrist measurement for the toggle clasp bracelet. You may need slightly less length if you use a smaller clasp.

You may also shorten the bracelet by removing one or more rows from the size 11/0 bead sections of the bracelet. If you remove one row from all eight of the seven-row sections, you can shorten the bracelet by ½" (1cm).

MATERIALS FOR A 9" (23cm) BRACELET

4lb FireLine fishing line or Nymo B or Silamide thread

Small copper toggle clasp—1

Size 11/0 bronze seed beads—5 to 6 grams

Size 8/0 copper-lined seed beads—108

Size 6/0 turquoise-lined seed beads—60

19mm × 19mm art glass bead with copper and turquoise center—1

TOOLS

Size 10 or 12 beading needle—1

Scissors

Straight pins

Glue

Weaving the First Half of the Rope

1 Cut as much thread as you think you can handle and single thread your needle. Tie the bar end of the toggle clasp onto the end of your thread with a square knot. Leave a 6" (15cm) tail, which you will work in later.

2 Thread on eight size 11/0 seed beads. Push them down against the toggle (Figure 1).

3 Pass your needle back toward the clasp, through the first six beads you added, and pull the thread through until you have the seventh and eighth beads tight against the first six (Figure 2).

4 Take your needle and pull slightly on the thread between these two beads so you have enough slack to arrange them upright so that they sit side by side astride the sixth bead (Figure 2). Tighten the thread.

5 Go through the clasp and up through the first five beads. Thread on three more beads. Pass the needle back through the first bead you threaded on and back through the five stem beads (Figure 3). Arrange the two beads as you did in the previous step.

6 Repeat this step one more time, being sure each time to pass through the clasp (Figure 4). You should have three sets of three beads, each made up of two beads sitting atop a single bead.

7 From the top, your beads should look like a six-bead circle (Figure 5).

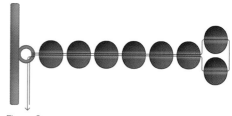

Figure 1

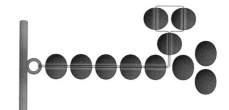

Figure 2

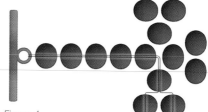

Figure 3

Figure 4

Figure 5

8 Pass your needle up through the five stem beads and one set of three beads, bringing it out on the left side of the two beads on top. Pick up two new beads and pass the needle down through the right bead.

9 Move the needle to the right and to the next three-bead set. Pass it up, through the left bead. Pick up two new beads and pass down through the right bead.

10 Move right to the third set and repeat. You should now have three sets of five beads.

11 Move the needle to the right and bring your needle up through the top left bead of the set again. Add two beads and go down the right bead.

12 Take your needle over to the next set and go up through the top left bead. Add two beads and pass through the top right bead. Repeat for the third set. You should have three sets with seven beads each.

13 Take your needle right and pass up through the top left bead, add two beads and pass through the top right bead.

14 Move the needle to the next set of beads and repeat. The joining thread between the two bead sets should always go straight across to the next set. Continue adding rows in this manner until you have five rows.

15 The sixth row is done with size 8/0 beads.

16 The seventh row is done with size 6/0 beads.

17 The eighth row is done with size 8/0 beads.

18 Rows 9 through 15 are done with size 11/0 beads.

19 Repeat steps 15 through 18 three more times.

20 Weave the next row with size 8/0 beads.

21 Weave the next row with size 6/0 beads.

Adding the Art Bead

1 Mark the last set of 8/0 beads you just added by running a straight pin through them.

2 Thread the art bead on your working thread.

3 To continue on the other side of the art bead, pick up two size 6/0 beads, and if the hole in the art bead is too big to keep them from sliding through, place a pin through them.

4 Pass back through the art bead and into the right side of the row you were last working in.

5 Pass the needle right to the next set of beads and up through the art bead. Pick up two beads, pass back through the art bead and continue in this manner until you have three sets of beads on the other side of the art bead.

6 When you come up through the art bead the next time, pass through the left side of one of the two bead sets, pick up two size 8/0 beads and pass through the right bead and back through the art bead.

7 Continue on this side of the art bead, as you have been doing. Come back up through the left bead of the second set and repeat. Do this for the third set as well, remembering to use size 8/0 beads for this row.

8 You will have to be very careful as you do this to keep the smaller beads from slipping through the larger hole of the art bead. Once you have two rows above the art bead, your third row (size 11/0 beads) will lock the beads together above the art bead. Remove any straight pins.

Finishing the Bracelet

1 Weave the second half of the rope following the *Weaving the First Half of the Rope* steps; for mirror results, reverse the order of steps.

2 To begin the final row, pick up four 11/0 seed beads. Pass the needle through the circle end of the toggle clasp.

3 Pass the needle back through the four beads you picked up. Take the needle through the right side of the set and down through two beads. Move to the next set of beads.

4 Pick up one bead and pass the needle through the three-bead stem and around the clasp. Move the needle through the right two beads. Move to the third set of beads and repeat.

5 Continue working until you have joined the sets all around. Each time, you will go down the stem and around the clasp. Tie off the thread and secure with glue. If you need more length, add extra beads in the stem.

Flat Herringbone Band Bracelet

As I mentioned earlier, herringbone weaving is often started on a base of ladder stitch. Such is the case with this band bracelet. The two rows of dark teal beads on the beginning edge of the band form a ladder, off of which the rest of the band is woven. After the basic band was stitched, I decided it was a little "blah," so to spark it up, I added some seed bead embellishment on top. Turns out adding the embellishment also tightened up the weave. If you stitch with a tight tension like I do, that could cause your band to pucker slightly. In this case it caused the band to curve out slightly, which makes it look nicer on the arm. Always take advantage of happy accidents, I say.

Variation

Flat Herringbone Yellow & Lavender Bracelet

This bracelet is done in the same manner as the project, but I had no pattern in mind when I started. I just started weaving patterns and changed when I felt I needed a contrast. If I were to do it again, I would choose a matte bead and a shiny one, as these colors are so close in tonal value that they don't contrast as well as I would like.

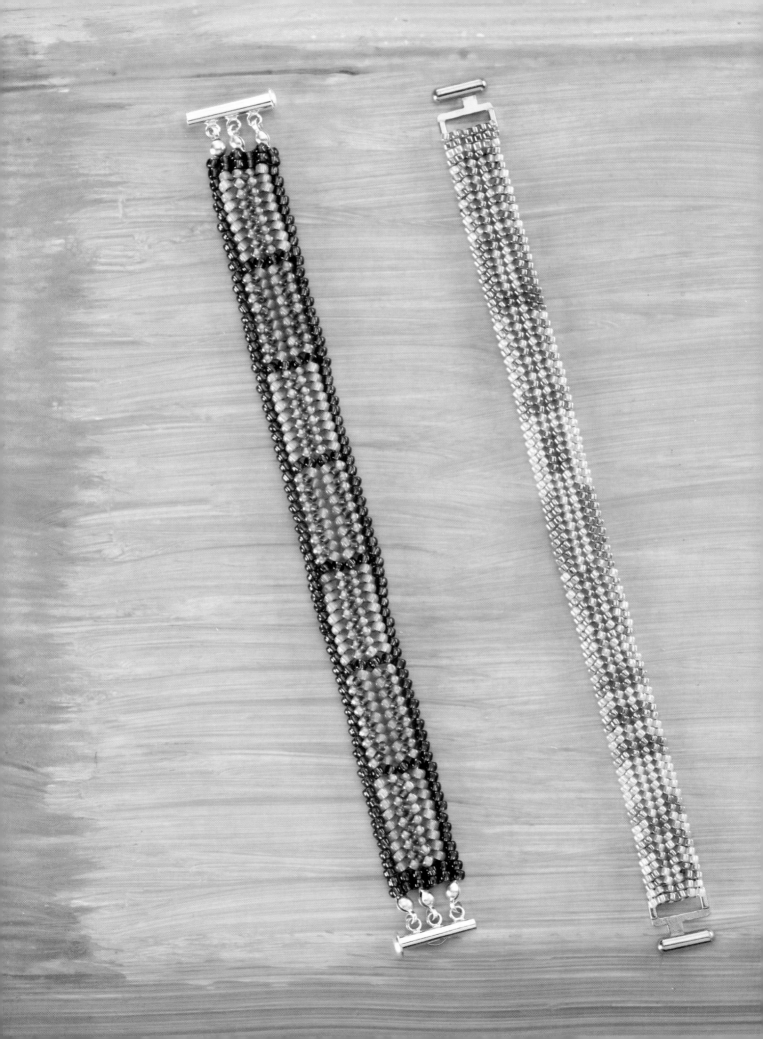

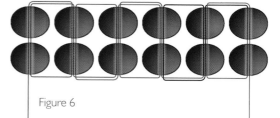

Figure 6

MATERIALS FOR A 7½" (19cm) BRACELET

6lb FireLine fishing line or .006" (.15mm) diameter WildFire beading thread

Size 8/0 dark teal silver-lined seed beads—5 grams

Size 8/0 pink gold-lined seed beads—5 grams

Size 8/0 light teal seed beads—5 grams

Size 11/0 dark teal silver-lined seed beads—1 gram

2mm crimp beads—6

Silver clamshell bead tips—6

3-strand slider clasp—1

TOOLS

Size 10 or 12 beading needle—1

Scissors

Figure 7

Weaving the Ladder

1 Refer to the instructions in *Chapter 1: The Sampler Bracelet* for the basic instructions on making a one-needle ladder band (page 24).

2 The ladder you will make to start this bracelet is two beads deep by six rows long (Figure 6). You may recall from previous mentions that when making a ladder, the beads in the ladder are referred to as "stacks." In this ladder, you will make a two-bead stack.

3 Pick up four size 8/0 dark teal beads, passing back through all four twice, pulling the beads around so they sit two by two (Figure 6, black thread).

4 The thread should be coming out of the bottom of the second stack. Pick up two more beads and pass back through the two just exited, pulling snug (Figure 6, red thread). Pass back through the two new beads again (Figure 6, red thread).

5 Continue following Figure 6 and adding two beads at a time until six rows are completed. Each additional row is illustrated with a different color line on the graphic. The thread should exit the final two beads at the bottom (Figure 6, magenta thread).

6 Bring the thread up from the bottom of the ladder to the top to start the herringbone weaving process. In order to accomplish this, pass the needle left to the second stack in from the end of the piece (Figure 7) and pass through the first bead in the stack only.

7 Then pass the needle back to the right and up through the second bead of the final stack (Figure 7). The ladder serves as rows 1 and 2 of the bracelet.

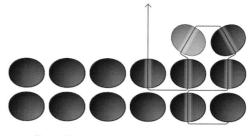

Figure 8

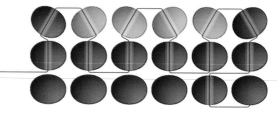

Figure 9

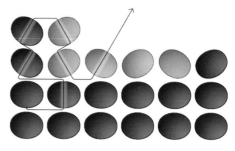

Figure 10

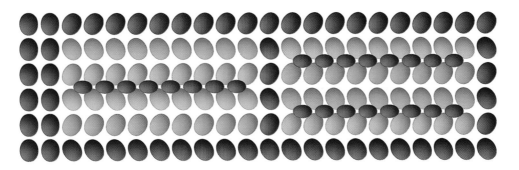

Figure 11

Starting the Herringbone Weaving

1. Pick up one dark teal and one pink bead. Pass back into the top teal bead of the second stack in from the end (Figure 8).

2. Pass the needle and thread left to the third stack in from the end and pass up through the top bead in the stack (Figure 8).

3. Pick up two light teal beads. Pass back into the top dark teal bead of the fourth stack in from the end (Figure 9).

4. Pass the needle and thread left to the fifth stack in from the end and pass up through the top bead in the stack (Figure 9).

5. Pick up one pink and one dark teal bead and pass the needle through the top dark teal bead of the sixth stack (Figure 9).

6. The thread should be pointing into the ladder. In order to bring it up to the top to start the fourth row, pass the needle to the right to the top bead of the fifth stack and pass up through this bead (Figure 10).

7. Pass the needle back to the left and pass it up through the dark teal bead in the first row of herringbone stitch (Figure 10).

8. To start the fourth row of the band, pick up one dark teal bead and one pink bead (Figure 10).

9. Pass the needle back through the pink bead just below (Figure 10).

10. Pass the needle right (Figure 10) and up through the light teal bead to start the next addition of beads.

11. The progression of the beading is shown in Figure 11. Repeat this double pattern three times. Then repeat the first half of the pattern once more.

12. Finish the band with two rows of dark teal beads. This may be done in herringbone or switch to a ladder stitch, if you prefer. Tie off the threads and trim the tails.

Adding the Embellishment (optional)

1. Bring a new thread into the work at one end of the band and bring it out of the end of a light teal bead. Pick up a size 11/0 seed bead.

2. Pass diagonally across the band into a light teal bead. Pick up another size 11/0 seed bead and pass diagonally across into a light teal bead again.

3. Continue in this manner until eight size 11/0 seed beads have been stitched down the center of the band between the light teal beads (Figure 12).

4. Referring to Figure 12, work down the band adding the embellishing beads. Tie off the thread and trim the tail.

5. Tie the threads off securely against a crimp bead. Trim the tails and close the clamshell. (See page 13 for clamshell instructions.)

6. Repeat steps 1 through 5 five more times to add all six clamshells.

7. Bend each clamshell bar on each end of the band around one of the loops in the sliding clasp.

Figure 12

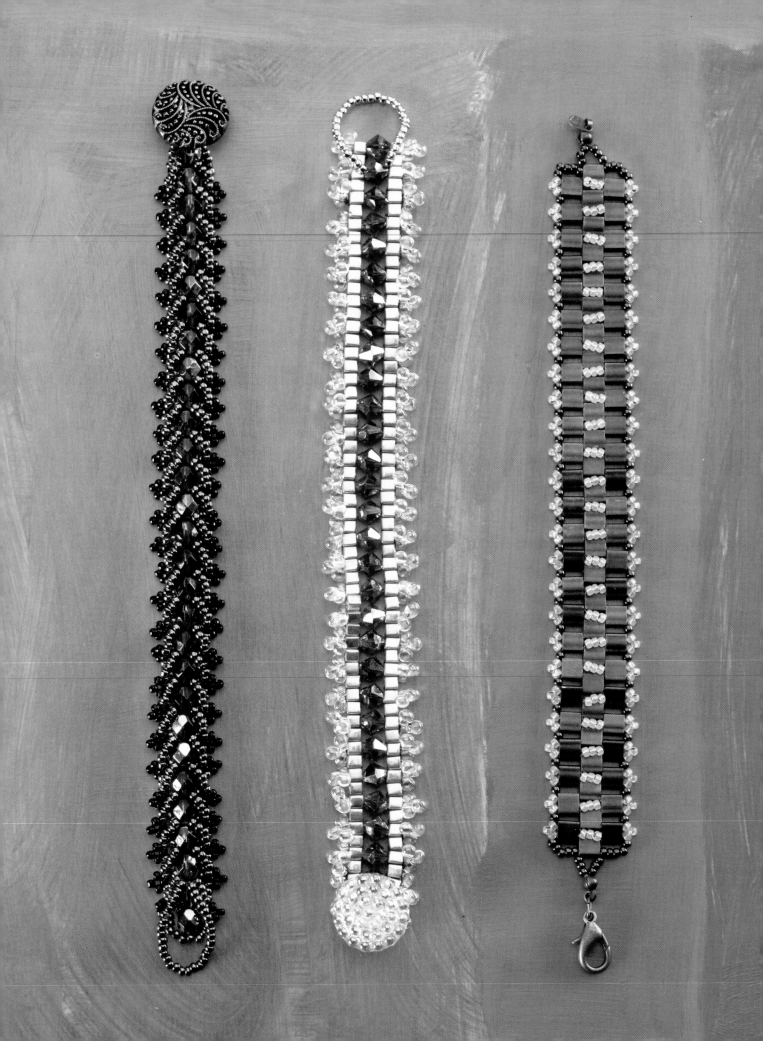

Chapter 9

Other Weaves

Sometimes weaving patterns don't always fall into a particular stitch category. Such is the case with the projects in this chapter. These projects utilize variations of the stitches or other weaves not covered in the book so far. The **Overlapping Loops Bracelet** is my take on an old pattern. The **Ladder Stitch Bracelet** was inspired by a chain and bead bracelet I found at a garage sale (though my finished project bears little resemblance to what inspired it). Finally, the **Tila Bead Bracelet** allowed me to play around with one of my favorite things to bead with—two-holed beads.

I hope these projects and the others in this book inspire you to strike out and try your own thing and discover ways to alter patterns to make them your own.

If there is a particular name for the stitch used in this bracelet, I have no idea what it is. I was taught the basic figure-eight stitch by Carole Best at the QIA beading group I attend, but the picot embellishment is my addition. Many new bead weaves are merely combinations of old stitches.

Variations

Overlapping Loops Bracelet in Crystals & Double Overlapping Loops Bracelet

The pink and green *Overlapping Loops Bracelet* features 6mm bicone crystals instead of fire polish beads. Because the crystals are slightly smaller than the fire polish beads, a seed bead was added between the crystals to lengthen the bead pattern so that the same fourteen-bead picot and loop weave could be used on the sides. Note the contrast of matte against shiny. It's a good design principle to use contrasting colors, finishes and textures; it adds depth to your work.

The *Double Overlapping Loops Bracelet* was done by first making the same basic band as in the project bracelet, with the exception of exchanging the picot for a 4mm crystal. Then a second band is woven in by making the outside loop as done for the project. Then, on the inside loop, pick up two seed beads. Then pass through two more seeds, a 4mm crystal and two more seeds of the inside loop of the first band. Then pick up two seeds on your needle and pass back through the center crystals. It's a little tricky to get started but makes a very rich-looking weave.

MATERIALS FOR A 7½" (19cm) BRACELET

8lb FireLine fishing line

6mm fire polish beads—29

Size 11/0 seed beads (major color)—6 to 7 grams

Size 11/0 seed beads (minor color)—2 to 3 grams

⅝" (16mm) shank button—1

TOOLS

Size 10 beading needle—1

Scissors

Glue (optional)

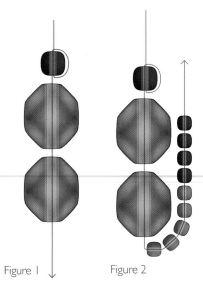

Figure 1   Figure 2

Making the Band

1 Cut as much thread as you can handle, and single thread the needle. A couple of yards (or meters) should make a bracelet of average length.

2 Tie a waste bead on the end of the thread, leaving a 10" (25cm) tail. Pick up two of the 6mm beads, as shown in Figure 1.

3 Pick up five of the major color seed beads and four of the minor color seed beads, as shown in Figure 2.

4 Loop the thread around and pass it back through the first minor color seed bead you picked up, making a loop, as shown in Figure 3. Pull the thread tight and keep the tension snug.

5 Refer to Figure 4, and pick up five more major color seed beads.

6 Pass through the two 6mm beads, as shown in Figure 5.

7 Repeat steps 3 through 6 on the other side, as shown in Figure 6. Keep one set of beads on each side of the 6mm beads, as shown.

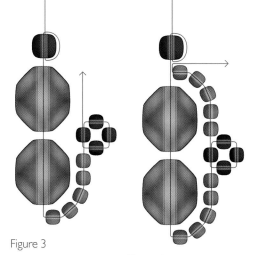

Figure 3

Figure 4

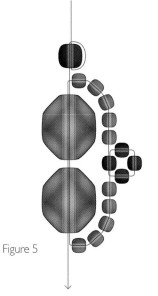

Figure 5

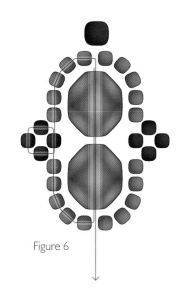

Figure 6

8 Pick up one 6mm bead, as shown in Figure 7.

9 Repeat steps 3 through 6, as shown in Figure 8, on the right side of the 6mm beads.

10 Repeat steps 3 through 6, as shown in Figure 9, on the left side of the 6mm beads.

11 Continue down the band, adding one 6mm bead each time and adding the loops on each side of two 6mm beads. For a snug fit, weave the band one 6mm bead short of meeting around your wrist.

12 Keep the tension snug so no thread shows. It is very important to keep the bracelet facing the same way at all times, as loops are being made on top of loops; if you turn the bracelet over or get confused as to which side you are working from, the pattern is likely to be lost.

Adding the Closure

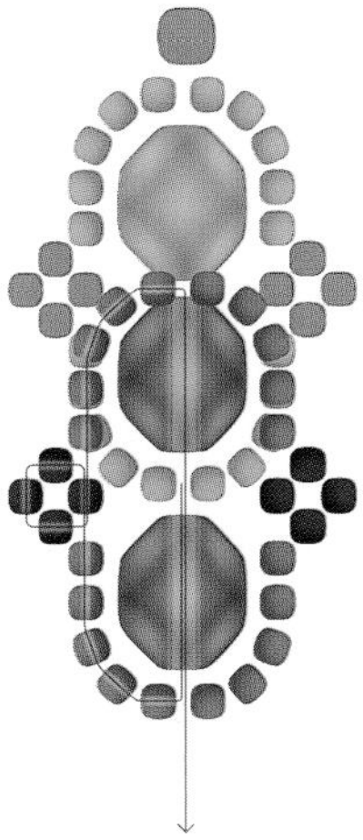

1 When the band is of the desired length, bring the needle out of the last 6mm bead and pick up three major color seed beads, the button and three more major color seed beads. Refer to Figure 10.

2 Pass around the beading and back through the button several times to reinforce.

3 Tie off the thread by working it through the beading and tying several half hitch knots as you go. Trim any excess thread.

4 On the other end, remove the waste bead and work through the beading until the needle comes out between the second and third 6mm beads. Refer to Figure 11.

5 Make a loop of beads long enough to pass easily over the button.

6 Pass the needle through the loops and beading several times to reinforce the loop.

7 Tie off the thread by working it through the beading and tying several half hitch knots as you go. Trim the excess thread. Glue if desired.

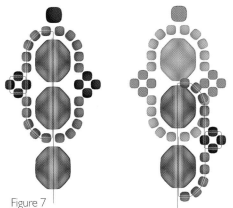

Figure 7

Figure 8

Figure 9

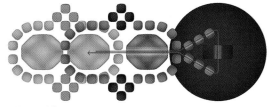

Figure 10

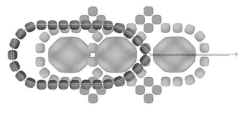

Figure 11

Ladder Stitch Bracelet

Ladder stitch has been used in a number of projects in this book as a starting place for other stitches. In this bracelet, the ladders are what make the bracelet possible. As I mentioned in the introduction to this chapter, the inspiration for this project is based on a chain and bead bracelet I found at a garage sale. The garage-sale find had a strand of box chain on either side. Beads were woven back and forth through the chain. My version uses ladders in place of the chain. I also dressed up my version with crystals, drop beads and a finished picot edge. There are many ways this project can be adapted—two of them are discussed in greater detail in the variations notes.

Variations

Blue & Black Ladder Stitch Bracelet

This bracelet is very similar to the project except the drop bead picot edge has been replaced with a peanut bead and a seed bead for a turning bead. I have also used peanut beads on either side of the center crystal.

Mini Cubes Ladder Stitch Bracelet

This delicate band uses mini cube beads for the continuous ladder which folds around and forms the loop for the button. The seed beads and 4mm bicone crystals are woven in and out along the length of the band, using every fourth cube bead.

Making the Ladders

1 Refer to *Chapter 1: The Sampler Bracelet*, page 24, for the basic instructions for making a one-needle ladder.

2 Weave two ladders with the 4mm gold cube beads, each fifty-nine beads long. Leave the ending tails hanging in case you need to make the bracelet longer.

3 Place the ladders one above the other on your work surface.

Figure 12

Weaving the Ladders Together

1 Single thread a needle with about 4' (1.2m) of thread. Tie a waste bead 8" (20cm) from the end of the thread.

2 Pass the needle through the first bead of the top ladder. Pick up a crystal bead and pass the needle through the first bead of the bottom ladder. Refer to Figure 12.

3 Pick up three drop beads and pass back through the lower ladder, the crystal and the upper ladder (Figure 12).

4 Pick up three drop beads (Figure 13), and pass back through the first gold bead on the top ladder.

5 Pass the needle right and up through the second gold bead (Figure 13) and right to the third gold bead and pass down through that bead, pick up a crystal and pass through the third bead in the bottom ladder.

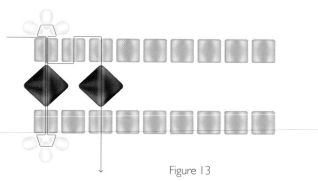

Figure 13

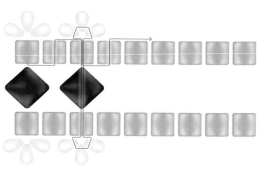

Figure 14

6 Pick up three drop beads (Figure 14), and pass back up through the lower ladder, crystal and upper ladder.

7 Pick up three drop beads, pass back through the third bead in the top ladder, pass over to the fourth bead and repeat steps 1 through 7 above (Figure 14).

8 Continue weaving in the manner described until you are within two beads of the end of each ladder.

9 If you need to add length, do so now. You will need to add two cube beads to each ladder for each additional pattern.

Finishing the Bracelet

1 When you get the length you need, work the needle to the end bead of the top pattern (Figure 15, black line).

2 Pass through the end bead of the top ladder, the shank of the button and the last bead of the lower ladder (Figure 15, black line).

3 Pick up three drop beads and pass back up through the beads and button that were added in step 2 (Figure 15).

4 Pick up three drop beads on the top edge of the bracelet and again pass the needle back through the beads and button pattern (Figure 15, red line).

5 Work back up and down through the beads and button a couple more times to reinforce.

6 Weave the thread tail into the bracelet, tying half hitch knots as you go. Trim the thread tail.

7 On the other end of the bracelet, work a new thread into the piece, bringing it out on one side of the center crystal bead (Figure 16).

8 Thread on enough of the size 11/0 gold seed beads to make a loop that will pass easily around the button (Figure 16).

9 Pass back through the loop of beads several times to reinforce.

10 Weave the thread tail into the bracelet, tying half hitch knots as you go. Trim the thread tail.

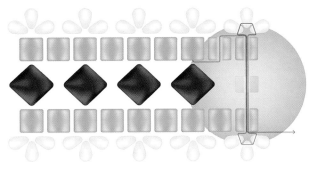

Figure 15

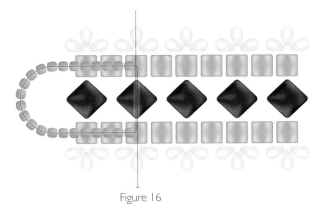

Figure 16

Tila Bead Bracelet

Tila beads are small 5mm square two-holed beads currently available in a limited range of colors. They are relatively new to the market and are manufactured by the Japanese bead company Miyuki. Being a lover of any bead with multiple holes, I couldn't wait to get my hands on some. Luckily, I found some before I started designing for this book.

This bracelet is created with two needles since it is done in a cross-weave pattern. The weave is a cross between a ladder stitch and a double-needle right-angle weave. I think you will find the stitch useful when designing patterns using two-holed beads.

Variations

Black Tila Bead Bracelet

This bracelet is a simplified version of the project, using just two rows of Tila beads in an up and down weave. The edges of the band are made the same as in the project.

Vintage Two-hole Bead Bracelet

This bracelet is woven in a nearly identical manner to the *Black Tila Bead Bracelet*, but because of the shape of the vintage beads, it looks entirely different. Two-hole beads are lots of fun to play with, and you can make all sorts of interesting designs with them.

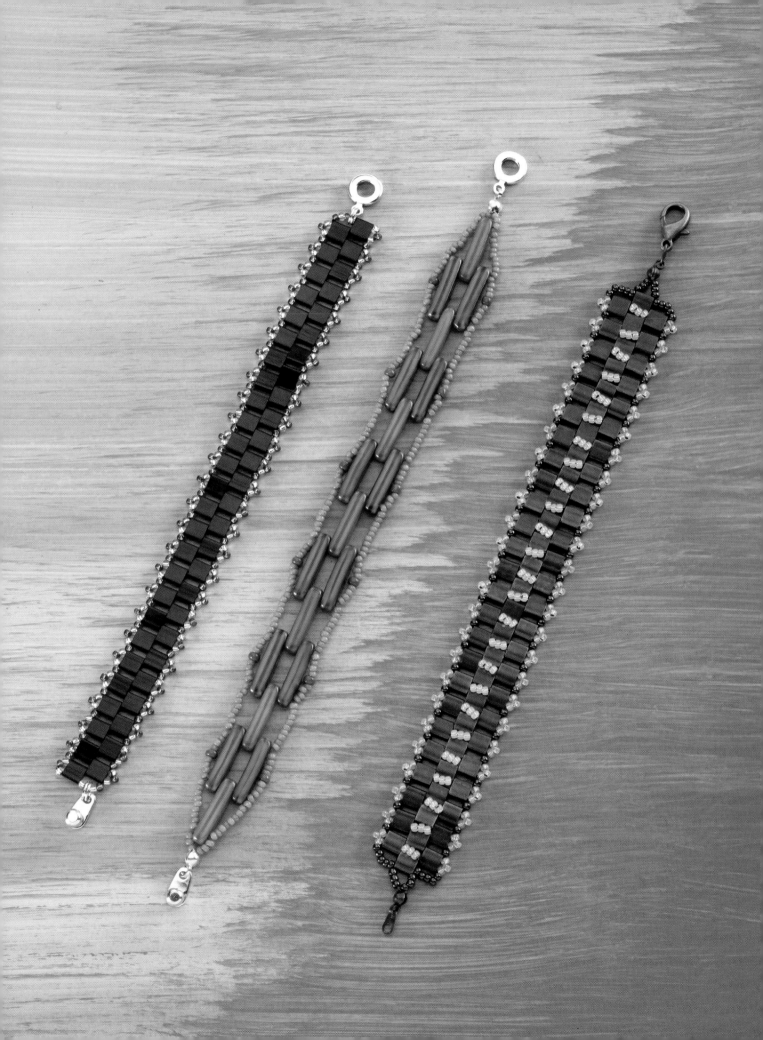

MATERIALS FOR AN 8" (20cm) BRACELET

6lb FireLine fishing line or .006" (.15mm) diameter WildFire beading thread

2mm crimp beads—2

Copper clamshell bead tips—2

Size 11/0 dark copper metallic seed beads—2 grams

Bronze Tila beads—76

Size 11/0 copper-lined white luster seed beads—3 grams

Copper lobster claw clasp—1

Copper clasp tag—1

Copper jump rings—1

TOOLS

Size 10 or 12 beading needles—2

Scissors

Chain-nose pliers

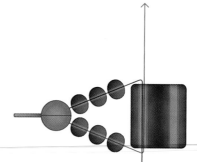

Figure 17

Starting the Bracelet

1 Cut 6' (1.8m) of thread and place a needle on each end, pulling the ends up. We will refer to the needles as the red needle and the black needle, referencing the lines on the illustrations for this part of the project.

2 Pick up a crimp bead on the red needle and center it on the thread. Pass the black needle through the crimp bead from the opposite direction, pulling snug.

3 Pass both needles through a clamshell bead tip from the inside to the outside. Use pliers to close the clamshell.

4 On each needle, pick up three dark copper seed beads (Figure 17).

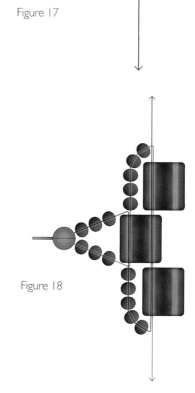

Figure 18

5 On the red needle, pick up a Tila bead using one hole. Pass the black needle through the same hole but from the opposite direction, and pull snug (Figure 17).

6 On the red needle, pick up five dark copper seed beads and one Tila bead (Figure 18, red line).

7 Pass the red needle through the second hole of the Tila bead from step 5 (Figure 18).

8 With the same (red) needle, pick up a second Tila bead (for a total of three Tila beads so far—Figure 18).

9 On the black needle, pick up five dark copper seed beads and pass through the three Tila beads from steps 6 through 8 (Figure 18).

10 On the red needle, pick up three copper-lined seed beads (Figure 19).

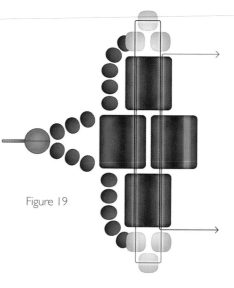

Figure 19

11 Pass the red needle through second hole of the top Tila bead (Figure 19). Pick up a new Tila bead and pass through the second hole of the bottom Tila bead.

12 Pick up three copper-lined seed beads on the black needle (Figure 19). Pass through the three Tila beads as shown (Figure 19).

13 With the red needle, pick up one dark copper seed bead and one Tila bead (Figure 20).

14 Pass through the second hole of the center Tila bead and pick up another Tila bead (Figure 20).

15 With the black needle, pick up one dark copper seed bead and pass through the three Tila beads as shown (Figure 20).

16 Continue following steps 10 through 15 until you have the length you need. End with a center Tila bead sticking out.

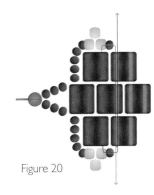

Figure 20

Finishing the Bracelet

1 To add the clasp on the other end, pick up five dark copper seed beads and pass the red needle through the second hole of the final, center Tila bead (Figure 21).

2 On the red needle, pick up three dark copper beads and pass through the underside of the clamshell bead tip (Figure 21). Let the thread hang.

3 Repeat steps 1 and 2 with the black needle (Figure 21).

4 Pick up a crimp bead with one needle. Tie off the threads against the crimp bead.

5 Trim the shortest thread. Leave the clamshell open. If you have enough thread left on the needle, you may use it for the final steps. If not, tie a new thread on the crimp bead.

6 To embellish the bracelet with copper-lined seed beads down the center of the band, pass your needle through the seed beads as shown (Figure 22) and up through the first two Tila beads.

7 Pick up three copper-lined seed beads and pass back through the lower Tila bead (Figure 22).

8 Pass through the dark copper seed on the edge of the bracelet and up through one Tila bead. Pick up three copper-lined seed beads (Figure 22).

9 Pass through two Tila beads (Figure 22).

10 Continue in this manner until you have a set of three seed beads over every space between the center-row Tila beads.

11 Work the thread through the beads, tying half hitch knots as you weave. Trim the thread end.

12 Close the clamshells. Bend the bars around each half of the clasp.

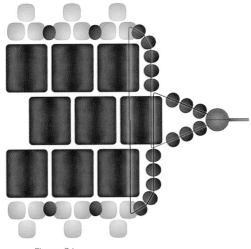

Figure 21

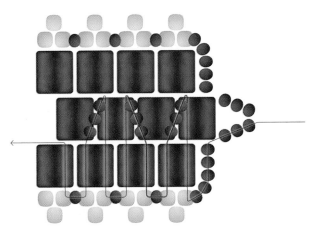

Figure 22

Carole Rodgers is an internationally known designer, author and teacher. She has been a professional designer for the past twenty-six years and had an extensive career in art education and art therapy prior to that. She is the sole author of ninety-nine needlework/crafting/beading pattern leaflets, hundreds of magazine articles and three full length beading books: **Beaded Jewelry with Found Objects** (2004), **Beading Basics** (2006) and **Beyond Beading Basics** (2009), all from Krause Publications. She has also been included in numerous multi-author hardcover books. She sells her line of self-published beading books and kits at retail shows.

Carole holds five patents for new product development. She teaches beading and needlework classes and has also served as a consultant to manufacturers in the craft industry. She has been actively involved in promoting crafts, beading and needlework in professional organizations and on national craft television programs. Her work has appeared in dozens of needlework and crafting magazines and nearly all national beading magazines.

She and her husband, LeRoy, also sell beads, gemstone cabochons and jewelry making supplies at retail bead and jewelry shows while they travel the United States in their RV. The couple has two daughters and two grandchildren.

Dedication

For my great family: LeRoy, Heather, Chris, Hunter, Renate and Rochelle. I love you all. Also for all my beading buddies at the QIA.

Acknowledgments

I would like to express my sincere gratitude to all the talented and creative people who have shared their knowledge and love of beading with me and through me to you, the reader. I appreciate their talents and their giving spirits.

I wish to thank the following companies for their help as well:

Artistic Bead

Beadalon

Hardies Beads & Jewelry

Stormcloud Trading

Wild Things Beads

Beacon Adhesives

Elka Designs

Morning Light Emporium

Tanya A. McGuire Designs

Lastly, I wish to thank the people at North Light Books for making this book happen: editor Kristy Conlin, designer Corrie Schaffeld, photographer Richard Deliantoni, and acquisitions editor Tonia Davenport.

16   15   14   13   5   4   3

DISTRIBUTED IN CANADA BY
FRASER DIRECT
100 Armstrong Avenue
Georgetown, ON, Canada L7G 5S4
Tel: (905) 877-4411

DISTRIBUTED IN THE U.K. AND EUROPE BY
F&W MEDIA INTERNATIONAL
Brunel House, Newton Abbot, Devon, TQ12 4PU, England
Tel: (+44) 1626 323200, Fax: (+44) 1626 323319
Email: enquiries@davidandcharles.co.uk

DISTRIBUTED IN AUSTRALIA BY
CAPRICORN LINK
P.O. Box 704, S. Windsor NSW, 2756
Australia
Tel: (02) 4577-3555

ISBN 13: 978-1-4403-1277-9
ISBN 10: 1-4403-1277-X
SRN: X9675

fw
media
www.fwmedia.com

Edited by Kristy Conlin
Designed by Corrie Schaffeld
Layout by Geoff Raker
Production coordinated by Greg Nock
Photography by Richard Deliantoni
Illustrations by Lindsay Quinter

Metric Conversion Chart

To convert	to	multiply by
Inches	Centimeters	2.54
Centimeters	Inches	0.4
Feet	Centimeters	30.5
Centimeters	Feet	0.03
Yards	Meters	0.9
Meters	Yards	1.1

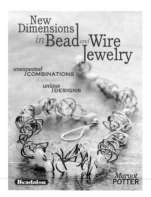